How To Dress for your Body Shape

A Complete Guide to Embracing Your Unique Silhouette

Print Book - ISBN: 978-1-7640606-0-8

eBook - ISBN: 978-1-7640606-1-5

First Edition

Published in Australia

Table of Contents

Dedication

For my beautiful daughter. May you always know your worth and walk confidently in the beauty God has given you.

Introduction

Welcome to Your Style Journey!

'How to dress for different body shapes' is a complete guide to assist you in finding the right outfits for your body shape. In a world where trends and idealised images often dictate style, it can be hard to find outfits that are right for you. No matter your body shape, there's a style that can accentuate your best assets and highlight your unique body form. Say goodbye to confusion and not knowing what to wear. You are in good hands and now have a personal stylist, fashion designer and multi-media artist in your corner. By the end of this book, you will feel confident in your style choices. Let's dive into this fun journey of discovery, creativity, and empowered dressing together!

Why This Book?

You might be wondering, 'Why should I think about my body shape when I get dressed?' Great question! Dressing for your body is about enhancing, balancing, and choosing outfits that feel both comfortable and aligned with who you are. The laws of physics, mathematics, design and art enable movement, precise calculations, functionality and creativity that enhance our daily lives every day and help us to advance our knowledge to live better, more efficient lives. Knowing the right clothing for your body shape helps you to move better, saves you time and money, and helps you to look your best! Although I want you to look your best, I want to make sure you understand that good style is not a fluke, but a calculated choice in any body shape, putting an end to guesswork, wrong purchases and wardrobe malfunctions, especially if like me, your life is full of mother and home duties, work and social events.

One of the most critical elements of choosing clothing is fit. Our minds automatically go to sizing when we think about clothing fitting us right; however, although wearing the right size is important to choosing the right outfit, we usually overlook another critical element of having the right fitting outfit, which is shape. Our body shape.

If we choose clothing that primarily considers our body shape, we find that sizing becomes more fluid. For example, because I am aware of my body shape, I can wear a top that is two sizes larger and one size smaller, as long as it flatters the shape of my body. I get compliments
and people wanting to know where I got my clothing from when I follow the rule of dressing for my body shape; however, when I wear the right size that does not suit my body shape, I don't have the same reaction from others, and I feel less confident in my outfit choice.

Understanding your body shape is like having a map that guides you toward the styles that help you shine and strengthen your knowledge of your unique style. This book isn't about restricting your options; it's about *expanding* them. With the knowledge of which clothing pieces suit you best, you will find shopping, getting your wardrobe organised, and getting dressed becoming a more positive experience of self-affirmation and creativity.

Fashion has long been an expression of identity, personality, and even mood. With a sustainable and streamlined approach to choosing your outfits, this complete guide will help you understand your body shape and choose the best outfits tailored to you. Having this book in your fashion and style arsenal will help you unlock the potential of your wardrobe and elevate your style and fashion with confidence.

How to Use This Book

Each chapter of this book dives into one of the five body shapes, providing:

- **Guidance on classic styling tips**: These are timeless principles that flatter each body shape, helping you look your best on any occasion.

- **Current trends and how to incorporate them**: Fashion is always evolving, and here you'll find ways to work in fresh styles that complement your body shape.

- **Visual examples**: From classic combinations to trend-driven outfits, I have provided illustrations of looks to demonstrate key styling tips. These illustrations make it easier to visualise what works best for your body shape.

We'll also explore fabric choices, colour theory, and accessory styling so that every piece of your outfit, from your clothing to your jewellery, works in harmony. In Chapter 8, I offer tips on building a body-type-friendly capsule wardrobe, creating a sustainable and efficient foundation that keeps you stylish and organised season after season. I also offer an appendix that works as a handy toolkit refresher for your convenience! A separate mini shopping guide is also available for purchase on my website or available free of charge for customers who have purchased this book. Just take a picture of your copy of this book and send it to support@stylebyaudra.com when requesting a copy. This shopping guide is essential if you would like to create an organised capsule wardrobe that celebrates your body shape.

Throughout this guide, you'll find practical, easy-to-apply advice, and yes, lots of fun! Finding your unique style should be fun, allowing you to experiment without pressure. This guide is here to give you the tools you need to make informed style choices while still letting your creativity lead the way.

Meet the Body Shapes

We're all built differently, and that's what makes fashion so exciting and each of us so unique! In this book, we'll explore five classic body shapes: Apple body shape, pear body shape, athletic body shape, hourglass body shape, and strawberry body shape. These shapes offer a starting point, not rigid boxes, where each body shape brings its own strengths and unique beauty. Here is a brief introduction to the body shapes discussed in this book:

1. **Apple Body Shape**: This body shape often features broader shoulders and a fuller bust, with slimmer hips and legs. Most ladies with this shape shine in outfits that elongate and bring balance to the midsection.

2. **Pear Body Shape**: With narrower shoulders and a wider hip area, most ladies with a pear body shape can enjoy creating balance by drawing the eye upward and celebrating curves with soft, flowy fabrics.

3. **Hourglass Body Shape**: A balanced bust and hips with a naturally defined waist make this body shape ideal for fitted styles that highlight curves. Ladies with the hourglass body shape stand out in many clothing styles.

4. **Athletic Body Shape**: With similar measurements across the shoulders, waist, and hips, ladies with athletic body shapes can play with volume, layering, and bold prints to create shape and dimension.

5. **Strawberry Body Shape**: Broader shoulders paired with slimmer hips make this body shape strikingly proportioned. Outfits that bring balance to the lower body, like wide-leg pants or A-line skirts, help to accentuate this body shape.

Each of these shapes has endless styling potential, and throughout this guide, we'll explore classic and current trends that can enhance your wardrobe.

Fashion as an Empowering Tool

Having a sense of personal style isn't about wearing the best brands. It is about creating your own unique brand that celebrates your personal taste in style. It is about feeling empowered, confident and motivated in your second skin, your clothing. Style is a shared expression of personal taste. It is a method of communication between ourselves and our environments. Our style choices both affect and reflect our preferences and create a silent dialogue within our spheres of influence. Personal style is a great way to create and build our personal brand, whether we are in business or not. It helps us communicate our desires and creates a perception of who we are and what we are about. Style is a powerful medium of communication.

The way we dress influences our confidence, affects how we present ourselves, and even impacts our mood. Imagine walking into a room knowing you look *amazing*. You're dressed in something that fits your personality, flatters your body, and makes you feel unstoppable. That's the kind of personal style we're talking about here. By understanding your body shape and styling accordingly, you're not just creating a look; you're building confidence, presence and a language that shapes your reality. Remember, dressing for your body type isn't about fitting a standard; it's about better defining your identity and enhancing your personal brand. It's about seeing the power in your unique figure and using style to enhance and express your personality and brand.

The beauty of understanding fashion and style in this way allows you to be selective and purposeful in how you shop and what you wear, embracing classic wardrobe staples while experimenting with current trends. Being clear about your personal style enables you to develop more sustainable style and fashion practices, reduce waste, use resources more effectively and save time. Understanding that the right 'fit' is key to selecting outfits that truly work for you, and that fit goes beyond sizing to align with your unique body shape, you can feel empowered and confident in your journey of dressing well for your body shape. With the guidance of this book, you'll be able to confidently choose clothing that flatters your figure and assists you in building the personal style brand you've always envisioned!

Embracing Body Positivity

Every woman's body is a masterpiece, *'fearfully and wonderfully made'*, and your personal style highlights your unique body, celebrating you. Whether you're looking for professional polish, casual confidence, or just want to make shopping for clothes and getting dressed easier, know that this book is the right place to start.

Together, let's explore how dressing well for your body shape can elevate your mood, boost your confidence, and simplify your wardrobe. Remember, style is personal, and what matters most is how you feel in what you wear.

You are invited to play around with looks and even try on other combinations once you have a good foundation on what works best for your unique body shape. Remember to join our online community and share your journey for a chance to be featured in our newsletter and social accounts.

So, get ready to open your closet to new possibilities, find your unique style, and step into each day with the assurance that your wardrobe beautifully reflects *your* personal style and brand, expresses your personality, and watch your confidence rise.

Let's start this journey together and have fun discovering the joy of dressing for the one-of-a-kind person that you are!

Chapter 1: Discovering Your Body Shape

Welcome to the beginning of your journey to a beautiful wardrobe that reflects and celebrates you! In this chapter, we're diving into the foundation of all great dressing. Understanding your body shape. Before we talk trends, before we mix and match outfits, and even before we consider colours and fabrics, the first step is getting to know the silhouette that makes you, *you*. By the end of this chapter, you'll have a clear picture of your body shape, the foundational knowledge and tools needed for building the perfect wardrobe to complement your body shape, and lots of tips for choosing looks that make you look and feel amazing. So, grab a tape measure, a mirror, and a pen and paper. Let's begin to unlock the secrets to your personalised style!

Why Your Shape Matters

Your body shape is like a unique blueprint. It's what sets you apart and gives you that unmistakable, beautiful visual identity. Learning to dress for your body shape doesn't mean sticking to rigid rules or only dressing in a certain way. It's about complementing your figure and creating outfits that accentuate your best features by designing well-thought-out outfits. Dressing for your body shape is the process of knowing and working with your natural lines and curves, highlighting what you love, and feeling confident in the process, and loving the results.

Remember, style is a medium of communication. What would you like to communicate about yourself, your personal brand and your tastes? Style and fashion are about highlighting and celebrating, even when your style preferences are minimalist. Knowing your unique body shape gives insight into the styles, cuts, and silhouettes that will elevate your look and confidence every time you look in the mirror. So, let's jump in and find out which best describes your uniquely beautiful silhouette! Remember, these categories are meant only as a guide, not a definition of your form. Only God can truly define your form!

Discover the Main Body Shapes

While everyone's body is beautifully unique, most women's figures generally fall into one of these five fundamental categories: Apple, pear, Athletic, hourglass, and strawberry Body Shape. Each body shape has its own unique beauty, and throughout this book, I have provided tools and tips you can tailor to help you choose the best outfits for your body shape while enjoying the process of dressing and organising your wardrobe better. Here's a breakdown of each body shape category discussed in this book:

Apple Body Shape

- **Description**: Women with an Apple body shape often have broader shoulders, a fuller bust, a less defined waist, and slimmer hips. Your legs may be one of your favourite features.

- **Style Goal**: Balance the top section of the body with the bottom by drawing attention to the lower body and creating a streamlined look.

Pear Body Shape

- **Description**: If you have a pear-shaped body, your hips are likely wider than your shoulders and bust, creating a natural curve on the lower section of your body. You may have a defined waist and a slender upper body.

- **Style Goal**: Bring the eye upward, balancing the hips by highlighting the upper body and enhancing the waist.

Athletic Body Shape

- **Description**: Women with an athletic or rectangular body shape have what is generally described as an 'athletic' build. They generally have similar measurements across their shoulders, waist, and hips, creating a straight silhouette.

- **Style Goal**: Create the impression of curves and dimension, using layering and varied textures to build shape and symmetry.

Hourglass Body Shape

- **Description**: The hourglass body shape features balanced shoulders and hips with a naturally defined waist. This is typically associated with curves in all the right places.

- **Style Goal**: Highlight and define the waist, letting your natural curves take centre stage. For a more elegant look, wear minimalistic and classic, feminine-style clothing. Ignore that advice if you prefer a more fun look.

Strawberry Body Shape

- **Description**: With broader shoulders and a narrower lower body, the strawberry body shape has a naturally strong presence. Shoulders are generally the widest point on the body, with the waist and hips being smaller in proportion.
- **Style Goal**: Balance the shoulders with the lower body by adding volume to the hips and avoiding excess width on top.

Understanding the Difference Between Apple & Strawberry Body Shapes

While both apple and strawberry body shapes share some common characteristics, such as broader shoulders and a narrower lower body, there are subtle distinctions that set them apart. Knowing these differences can help in selecting the most flattering styles for each body shape.

- **Apple Body Shape**: Typically characterised by a fuller bust and midsection with weight concentrated around the torso. Apple body shapes often have slimmer hips and longer legs, which can be standout features. The key styling focus is to create visual balance by enhancing the lower body and elongating the torso, thereby drawing attention away from the upper body, toward the lower body.

- **Strawberry Body Shape**: Characterised by broad shoulders and a more athletic build, this body shape often features a defined waist and slim hips. Styling for strawberry body shapes focuses on balancing the upper body's width by adding volume to the lower body. Suitable styles include A-line skirts and wide-leg pants, which help to create a proportional silhouette and draw attention to the waist.

Styling Tips for Each Body Shape:

- **Apple Body Shape**: Look for structured outerwear that adds definition at the waist, V-neck tops to elongate the torso, and A-line mini, mid-length or maxi skirts to create balance. Structured outerwear, such as tailored coats, jackets and blazers, is your ally.

- **Strawberry Body Shape**: Go for outfits that add volume to the lower body, such as skirts with ruffles or wide-leg pants. Simple, loosely fitting tops help avoid drawing extra attention to the shoulders.

Exploring Your Body Shape

How can you determine your body shape? It's quite simply discovered with a few simple measurements. You will need a measuring tape, a mirror and a pen with some paper. I recommend dedicating a notebook or journal to your styling journey. Once you have your tools ready, follow the steps below to identify which main body shape category your body features fit into.

1. **With a measuring tape**: Measure across your shoulders, bust, waist, and hips.
   - *Shoulders*: Measure across the widest part of your shoulders.
   - *Bust*: Wrap the tape around the fullest part of your bust.
   - *Waist*: Find the narrowest part of your waist, usually just above the belly button.
   - *Hips*: Measure around the fullest part of your hips.

2. **Compare Your Measurements**: Once you have these numbers written down, look at the proportions.

    o   If your shoulders are noticeably wider than your hips, you might have an apple body shape. (See the difference between apple and strawberry body shapes).

    o   If your hips are the widest point in your measurements, you may have a pear body shape.

    o   If your bust and hips measurements are close, having a well-defined waist, you probably have an Hourglass body shape.

    o   If your measurements are similar across the board, you likely have an athletic, (athletic) body shape.

    o   If your shoulders are wider and your waist and hips narrower, you most likely have a Strawberry body shape.

Tip: Complete the quiz online at **stylebyaudra.com** for more information and wardrobe organisational tools.

Don't worry about exact numbers! This is just to get a general sense of your proportions so that you can better understand which styles enhance your natural silhouette. Bear in mind that over time, our bodies change shape. Like mine, many women's bodies change shape after having children. Knowing your body shape helps you make purposeful choices with style and fashion that reflect your personal brand and celebrate how far you have come.

Common Myths About Body Shapes

It's easy to fall into the trap of thinking that some shapes are better than others. This is simply not true! Everybody's shape is beautiful and offers different opportunities for unique styling experiences. Here are a few myths we're debunking right now:

- **Myth #1: The hourglass body shape is the "ideal" body shape**

The truth is, there is no "ideal" body shape. All shapes are uniquely beautiful, and each has its own style strengths. Embracing the body shape you have helps you understand what works best for you and helps you shine in your chosen outfits. There's beauty to be found and accentuated in every silhouette!

- **Myth #2: You should "hide" parts of your body**

True style is about celebrating and highlighting our uniqueness, not hiding who we are. This book is all about exploring your unique body shape with confidence and helping you feel empowered in every outfit you choose.

- **Myth #3: Body shape is static.**

Our bodies can change over time, and that's perfectly normal! These tips are flexible and adaptable, so you can always find something that works for you, no matter where you are in life.

Celebrating Your Body Shape

By understanding your body shape, you are already one step closer to building a wardrobe that works *for* you, not against you. Every body shape has its advantages: Apple body shapes often have great, long legs and enviable busts, pear-shaped bodies rock the natural curves, athletic silhouettes can play with volume like no other, hourglass body shapes show off balanced proportions, and strawberry-shaped bodies can bring boldness to every outfit.

As we move through this book, remember that these categories are just tools for discovering which outfits best suit you. They don't define you. They're here to help you navigate style options, making it easier to identify what might look and feel great on you. If you want to break the 'rules' or try something unexpected, go for it! Style is personal, and fashion is meant to be fun.

Visual Guide: Inspiration

See how different body shapes are celebrated with a variety of styles. Take a moment to explore the style illustrations on the next pages, where each body type is represented in a classic, flattering silhouette. Notice how the clothing works with the body's natural lines, enhancing balance and flow. As you look through, consider what resonates with you. Maybe there's a silhouette or style that catches your eye!

Figure 1

Figure 2

Figure 3

Figure 4

Ready for the Next Step?

Now that you know your body shape, you're ready to start exploring styles that complement your figure. In the chapters that follow, we'll dive into each body shape and provide practical styling tips, classic and trendy outfit examples, and visual guides to inspire you. Remember, this isn't about following strict rules; it's about creating looks that accentuate your unique beauty. Whether you're a classic dresser, love keeping up with the latest trends, or are a bit of both, like me, you'll find ideas that fit your body, your lifestyle, and your personality.

Here's to the start of a beautiful adventure in discovering your personal style. Let's celebrate your unique beauty and empower you to dress in ways that make you feel confident, comfortable, and '*uniquely designed*' because you are a masterpiece.

Let's start exploring the styles that celebrate you.

Chapter 2: Dressing for Apple Body Shapes

Welcome to your personal styling guide for Apple body shapes! If you've discovered that your shoulders are broader than your hips, your bust is fuller, and your waistline is less defined, you're in great company. Celebrities like Catherine Zeta Jones and Jennifer Hudson have mastered the art of dressing their Apple body shapes well, creating beautiful, balanced looks that flatter their figures. In this chapter, we'll dive into classic styling tips, current trends, and outfit ideas to make the most of your apple body shape, and, most importantly, to make dressing up fun and confidence-boosting!

Understanding the Apple body shape

The Apple body shape, also sometimes called the Strawberry, typically has:

- **Broader Shoulders and Bust**: Your upper body is the widest part, creating a strong, beautiful frame.

- **Less Defined Waist**: The midsection might be softer and more rounded, with less natural definition.

- **Slimmer Hips and Legs**: You might find your legs are naturally toned, making them a feature to show off!

Apple shapes look fabulous in styles that bring balance to the upper and lower body by elongating the midsection and drawing attention to the lower body.

Classic Tips for Dressing Apple Body Shapes

Let's start with the timeless styling principles that work beautifully for Apple shapes. These tips never go out of style, giving you a framework you can always rely on.

1. **Embrace V-Necks and Scoop Necks**
   - **Why**: V-neck and scoop neck tops create a vertical line down your torso, drawing the eye downward and elongating your body shape.

- Try This: V-neck blouses, wrap tops, or scoop-necked tees that elongate and bring balance to your look.

2. **Highlight Your Lower Body**
   - **Why**: Apple body shapes often have stunning legs and a defined lower body. Shorter hemlines or tailored pants help highlight the lower section of your body.

   - **Try This**: Tailored pants or high-waisted shorts that bring focus to your legs. Pair them with a slightly loose or flowy top for a balanced look.

3. **Choose A-Line Dresses and Skirts**
   - **Why**: A-line silhouettes that skim over the midsection and gradually flare out add balance to your body shape.

   - **Try This**: A classic A-line dress or skirt with a nipped waist that flares gently, creating an effortless flow.

4. **Structured Outerwear is Your Friend**
   - **Why**: Tailored blazers, jackets, and coats add definition around the shoulders and waist, lending structure to your body shape.

   - **Try This**: Look for blazers and jackets that have a nipped waist or an adjustable belt that aligns with the narrowest point above your belly button, where you took your measurements. These pieces can create a balanced, polished look.

5. **Go for Darker, Solid Colours on Top**
   - **Why**: Dark colours on your upper body help create a balanced look, while lighter or brighter colours on the bottom draw attention downward.

   - **Try This**: Try pairing a black or navy top with a light or bold, printed skirt or pants to shift focus away from the shoulders and bring attention to your lower body.

Current Trends for Dressing Apple Body Shapes

Fashion trends are ever evolving, and incorporating them into your wardrobe is a great way to keep things fresh and exciting. Let's look at some of today's hottest styles and how they work beautifully for Apple shapes.

1. **Oversized Blazers and Jackets**
   - **Why**: Oversized outerwear is not only on-trend, but it also helps to balance your outfit by adding intentional volume without clinging.

   - **Try This**: An oversized blazer over a fitted tee and straight or boyfriend jeans creates a stylish contrast that highlights your legs and adds structure up top.

2. **High-Waisted, Tailored Pants**
   - **Why**: High-waisted, tailored, loose and baggy pants define the waist and add volume to the lower body, balancing out broader shoulders.

   - **Try This**: High waist, loose or baggy jeans. Also, try tailored, high-waist or wide-leg pants in a light colour, or bright pattern. Pair with a French tucked-in top for a trendy, balanced look.

3. **Statement Tops with Subtle Details**
   - **Why**: Simplifying the upper section of your body minimises the appearance of bulk and draws attention away from the broader shoulders. Structured tops with clean lines and minimal detail help elongate the torso and balance the silhouette.

   - **Try This**: opt for tops with a tailored fit and minimal detailing. A well-fitted blazer or a simple, sleek blouse with vertical seams can create a flattering look without adding volume. Avoid overly embellished or puffy sleeves, which might emphasise the upper body. Instead, select garments that enhance your natural look while maintaining a clean and elegant profile.

Expert Tip: Beautiful buttons make a statement while elongating your body shape.

4. **Layered Looks**
   o **Why**: Layering can add depth to an outfit, creating interesting lines that elongate the body and shift focus away from the midsection.

   o **Try This**: Try layering a fitted longline cardigan over a monochrome outfit to create a lengthening effect.

   o **Expert Tip:** With the right colours, varying hemline lengths, such as a long-line cardigan over a monochrome outfit or a vest under a jacket or over a blouse, can draw attention to the lower body, adding flair and accentuating your style.

5. **Asymmetrical Hems**
   o **Why**: Asymmetrical hems create visual movement, drawing the eye downward and elongating your silhouette.

   o **Try This**: Asymmetrical skirts or wrap dresses with slanted hems add a trendy, unexpected flair.

Before & After Styling Exercises

Sometimes, small changes make all the difference! Below, you'll find examples showing an Apple before and after applying these styling techniques:

1. **From Boxy to Balanced**: See how swapping a shapeless top for a structured blazer transforms the look by defining the waist and adding polish.

2. **From Clingy to Flattering**: Compare an ill-fitting dress with a tailored A-line dress, which enhances the waist and provides flow.

3. **From Top-Heavy to Proportional**: Observe how pairing a darker, solid top with a bright coloured high-waisted pair of pants can help bring balance and shift focus to the lower body.

Share Your Journey with Us

Share your experience with us to help guide other Apple body-shaped readers. Head to stylebyaudra.com and sign up for a free membership, which will enable you to join our community, build a style profile and share your journey with us! You will also be the first to know of any updates, brand collaborations and styling workshops coming to a city near you. Let's make our learning fun and interactive!

Embracing Your Body Shape

Apple shapes bring a powerful, graceful presence to fashion, with broad shoulders that give a naturally elegant frame. Don't shy away from showing off those great legs or experimenting with different fits and styles. Dressing for your apple body shape is about making choices that bring you joy and confidence, choosing clothes that make *you* feel fabulous.

If you feel inspired to try something new, go for it! Fashion is an adventure, and with each outfit, you're exploring new ways to express who you are. Whether you're in the mood for classic elegance or a trendy look, remember that your body shape is a beautiful part of what makes you unique.

Visual Inspiration Gallery

Look at the visual inspiration examples on the next page, tailored for Apple shapes. This section brings the styling tips to life, showcasing how A-line dresses, wide-leg trousers, and statement outerwear work together to enhance your silhouette. Each outfit reflects a thoughtful blend of classic and modern elements, encouraging you to experiment with colours, fabrics, and cuts that celebrate your unique body shape. Use these outfit demonstrations as creative inspirations to imagine new combinations and build a wardrobe that feels beautiful, confident, and perfectly you.

The following images are described from top to bottom, left to right, on each row.

• Look #1: Elegant Earth Tones in Motion

A warm rust overcoat paired with a soft blush A-line midi skirt creates a graceful, elongating silhouette. The V-neck blouse brings vertical balance, while the structured coat and soft brown accessories draw attention downward. This look balances the torso while enhancing the legs, a timeless favourite for Apple shapes.

• Look #2: Colour-Blocked Contemporary Chic

A longline neutral coat and deep V-neck slate blouse elongate the upper body, while two-tone trousers add visual interest and shift attention to the legs. The rounded handbag introduces soft volume below the waist, bringing modern balance to the silhouette with an artistic twist.

• Look #3: Soft Neutrals for Clean Definition

A tailored dark brown blazer over a crisp white scoop-neck top defines the shoulder line without adding bulk. Paired with high-waisted, wide-leg tan trousers, this look redirects focus to the lower half. Pointed heels and a compact handbag complete this classic, polished outfit ideal for everyday styling.

• Look #4: Navy Statement Structure

This striking ensemble features a navy A-line dress beneath a belted double-breasted coat, creating the illusion of a cinched waist. The metallic belt and accessories elevate the outfit, while heeled boots add length to the frame, an empowering and elegant cold-weather choice.

Figure 5

Figure 6

Figure 7

Figure 8

Apple Body Shape Style Tips

- **Go-To Outfit Formula**: Dark, fitted V-neck top + bright or patterned A-line skirt or wide-leg pants.

- **Key Tips**: Keep the upper body sleek with simple lines and add interest with fuller bottoms or bold colours on the lower section of your body.

- **Essential Fabrics**: Lightweight, flowing fabrics on top, paired with structured bottoms to create balance.

Ready for the Next Body shape?

Once you're comfortable with dressing your Apple body shape, feel free to move to the next chapter or return to these tips whenever you need a refresh. Every body shape in this book has its own unique strengths and endless styling possibilities, so have fun exploring!

Here's to the powerful, balanced, and chic styles that enhance the Apple body shape. Let's keep the fun going and dive into the next chapter, where we'll explore all the fantastic ways to dress the *Pear body* shape!

Chapter 3: Dressing for Pear Body Shapes

Welcome, Pear shapes! If you've got a smaller upper body, defined waist, and hips that curve beautifully, you're a classic Pear (also called the triangle body shape). Many iconic beauties share your body shape, like Jennifer Aniston, Rihanna, and Shakira's hips don't lie! These celebrities know how to make the best of their body shape. This chapter is all about showing off your best features, creating balance, and having fun with fashion. With a few tips and styling secrets, you'll have a wardrobe that works effortlessly with your body shape and highlights what you love most about your body. Let's get ready to embrace and celebrate your stunning Pear silhouette!

Understanding the Pear Body shape

The Pear body shape, also known as the Triangle, typically has:

- **Wider Hips and Thighs**: Your hips are wider than your shoulders and bust, giving you that natural, beautiful curve.

- **Narrower Shoulders and Bust**: Your upper body may be smaller than your lower body, giving you lots of options to play with proportions.

- **Defined Waist**: Pear shapes usually have a clearly defined waist, a fantastic feature to highlight!

Pear shapes look fabulous in styles that bring attention upward to the shoulders and bust, enhance the waist, and create balance with the hips. This is perfect for showing off your curves and using layers, colours, and textures to add interest to your look.

Classic Tips for Dressing Pear Body Shapes

Let's start with some timeless styling principles that have been proven to work beautifully for Pear shapes. These classic tips will guide you toward outfits that bring balance, highlight your waist, and let your unique shine.

1. **Bring Attention Upward with Detailed Tops**

o **Why**: Adding details on top, like embellishments, prints, or bright colours, draws the eye upward and balances the width of your hips.

o **Try This**: Choose tops with ruffles, puff sleeves, or statement collars. Light colours and bold patterns also work beautifully to add interest.

2. **Opt for A-Line Skirts and Dresses**

o **Why**: A-line skirts and dresses skim over the hips and gently flare out, creating a lovely balance with your upper body.

o **Try This**: Knee-length A-line dresses in solid colours or subtle prints that flow gracefully from your waist for an effortlessly flattering look.

3. **Go Dark and Simple on the Bottom**

o **Why**: Darker shades on the lower body naturally minimise the hips and thighs, creating a streamlined, balanced look.

o **Try This**: Stick with darker jeans or trousers, or wear skirts in navy, black, or earth tones that don't add extra volume to the lower section of your body.

4. **Highlight Your Waist**

o **Why**: Your defined waist is one of your best features, and accentuating it adds to your silhouette.

o **Try This**: Look for tops that cinch at the waist, wrap dresses, and high-waisted pants. Belts are a great accessory for Pear shapes, as they emphasise your natural waistline.

5. **Choose Statement Outerwear**

o **Why**: Jackets and blazers with embellished collars and shoulders add interest to your upper body and create visual balance. Tailored outerwear enhances your silhouette by defining your waist and complementing your proportions, offering a polished, proportional look.

o **Try This**: Look for tailored jackets with shoulder details, like epaulettes, lapels with unique cuts or collar blocking around the collar. Subtle padding can help broaden your shoulders in a way that balances the lower body. A cinched waistline or belt provides definition and structure.

o **Expert Tip:** Avoid details and embellishments below the waistline.

Current Trends for Dressing Pear Shapes

Who says you can't enjoy the latest trends? Modern styles offer so many fun options for pear shapes, from high-waisted pants that celebrate your waist to statement tops that bring attention upward. Let's dive into some of the hottest trends and see how they work perfectly with your body shape.

1. **High-Waisted Wide-Leg Pants**
   o **Why**: High-waisted pants define the waist and lengthen the legs, while the wide-leg cut creates balance with the hips.

   o **Try This**: Pair wide-leg trousers in a dark colour with a tucked-in, light-coloured blouse or crop top to accentuate your waist and balanced proportions.

2. **Puff Sleeves and Statement Shoulders**
   o **Why**: Puff sleeves and structured shoulders are on-trend and work beautifully for Pear shapes by adding volume and interest to the upper body.

   o **Try This**: Opt for a puff-sleeved blouse or a top with shoulder detailing to bring focus upward and create symmetry.

3. **Colour Blocking**
   o **Why**: Colour blocking is a fun trend that lets you play with colours in a way that balances your silhouette.

o **Try This**: Choose tops in lighter or brighter colours paired with darker, solid-coloured bottoms. Colour blocking draws attention to the upper body, balancing your body shape.

4. **Asymmetrical Necklines**
   o **Why**: Asymmetrical necklines are both trendy and flattering, as they add unique visual interest to the upper body.

   o **Try This**: Look for one-shoulder tops or dresses with asymmetrical necklines to add flair to the upper section of your body while balancing out your proportions.

Before & After Styling Exercises

Sometimes, even small changes can make a big difference. Here are a few before-and-after examples to illustrate how specific styling adjustments can transform an outfit:

1. **From Top-Heavy to Balanced**: See how switching from a fitted, solid-coloured top to a puff-sleeved blouse adds volume to the upper body, balancing out the hips and creating a more proportionate look.

2. **From Ill-Fitting to Flattering**: Compare how a loosely fitted dress looks with and without a belt. Cinching the waist emphasises your curves and defines your body shape.

3. **From Overwhelming to Balanced Layers**: Notice how a long cardigan with a fitted top underneath draws the eye downward, creating balance without overwhelming the hips.

Share Your Journey with Us

Share your experience with us to help guide other Pear body-shaped readers. Head to stylebyaudra.com and sign up for a free membership, which will enable you to join our community, build a style profile and share your journey with us! You will also be the first to know of any updates, brand collaborations and styling workshops coming to a city near you. Let's make our learning fun and interactive!

Embracing Your Body Shape

As a Pear body shape, you have a wonderfully natural curve that's both feminine and graceful. By drawing attention to your upper body, emphasising your waist, and balancing your hips, you can create endless looks that highlight the best of your body shape. And remember, these are guidelines, not rules! Style is all about expression, so feel free to mix things up and experiment with what feels right for you.

Your curves are an asset and dressing them in ways that make you feel empowered is what fashion is all about. Whether you're heading to work, going out with friends, or relaxing at home, dressing for your body shape is a way to embrace and celebrate the person you are.

Visual Inspiration Gallery

Explore a variety of looks designed for Pear shapes. From A-line dresses to puff-sleeve tops, these visuals offer inspiration for making the most of your unique silhouette. Use these ideas as a springboard for creating outfits that feel just right for you.

To make these styling tips come to life, let's look at some outfit combinations designed specifically for Pear shapes. Each example highlights how classic pieces, and trendy elements can work together to create a look that's balanced, fun, and flattering. Reference: Outfit Layout (Top to Bottom, Left to Right)

Look #1: Soft Blue Contrast and Shine

A baby blue A-line dress cinched at the waist is layered with a structured pale grey blazer, creating visual lift at the shoulders and definition at the waist. Tall silver boots elongate the legs and ground the look, offering a fresh twist that draws attention upward for pear-shaped bodies.

Look #2: Sleek and Elongated Lines

High-waisted black wide-leg trousers paired with a cropped orange top bring vibrant attention to the upper body. A longline charcoal cardigan adds length while balancing the hips, creating a strong vertical silhouette ideal for pears.

Look #3: Autumn Layers with Flow

A rich amber tiered maxi dress skims gracefully over the hips and thighs, while a cropped fringe jacket draws attention to the upper body. The soft structure at the top and fluidity below create balance, enhanced by mid-height boots that elongate the legs.

Look #4: Puff Sleeves and Neutral Tones

A soft puff-sleeved blouse adds volume to the upper body, while the deep grey cropped flare pants slim the hips and thighs. Pointed boots and a structured handbag finish the look with elegance, making it a balanced and modern choice for pear-shaped styling.

Figure 9

Figure 10

Figure 11

Figure 12

Pear Body Shape Style Tips

o **Go-To Outfit Formula**: Patterned or textured top + high-waisted tailored trousers in dark colours.

o **Key Tips**: Draw attention upward with interesting tops and keep the lower body streamlined to create balance.

o **Essential Fabrics**: Structured materials for bottoms and softer, eye-catching fabrics on top.

Ready for the Next Body shape?

Once you've got a handle on dressing for your Pear body shape, feel free to revisit these tips as often as you like. Each chapter in this book has unique insights for different body shapes, so feel free to explore and get inspired by styles across the board.

Now, let's move on to the next chapter and explore all the stylish possibilities for the **Hourglass body** shape!

Chapter 4: Dressing for Hourglass Body Shapes

Welcome to the style playground for the Hourglass body shape! If you've discovered that your shoulders and hips are balanced with a naturally defined waist, you're among fashion royalty. The hourglass body shape is often celebrated for its balance and curves, bringing to mind icons like Marilyn Monroe, Sophia Loren, and Salma Hayek. Knowing your body shape makes it easy to pull off looks that highlight your waist, enhance your curves, and embrace your silhouette with confidence.

Let's dive into the styling secrets that make the most of your Hourglass figure, from classic wardrobe staples to the latest trends. Get ready to enjoy every part of dressing up!

Understanding the Hourglass Body Shape

The hourglass body shape is often described as the '*ideal*' due to its proportional balance. Your body type is characterised by:

- **Balanced Shoulders and Hips**: Your shoulders and hips are similar in width, creating symmetry.

- **Defined Waist**: Your waist is noticeably narrower than your bust and hips, creating a natural curve that's ideal for highlighting.

- **Full Bust and Hips**: You may find that you have naturally fuller bust and hip areas, giving you an attractive, curvaceous body shape.

Hourglass figures look fabulous in outfits that hug the curves and define the waist. This body shape thrives in fitted, structured pieces that allow you to show off your figure without overwhelming it. Think tailored dresses, high-waisted pants, and classic, streamlined silhouettes that accentuate your natural lines.

Classic Tips for Dressing Hourglass Shapes

With the Hourglass body shape, there's a world of style possibilities that enhance your curves and highlight your waist. Here are some classic styling principles to keep in your fashion toolkit.

1. **Define the Waist**
   - **Why**: Your defined waist is one of your most beautiful features, and highlighting it brings balance to your figure.
   - **Try This**: Belted dresses, high-waisted pants, and wrap dresses that pull in at the waist are great options to create that iconic Hourglass outline.

   1. **Embrace Fitted Clothing**
   - **Why**: Tailored, fitted styles hug your curves in all the right places, showcasing your figure without adding bulk.

   - **Try This**: Opt for tops and dresses that are slightly fitted at the waist and hip area, avoiding overly loose or boxy shapes that hide your curves.

   2. **Go for V-Necks and Scoop Necks**
   - **Why**: These necklines elongate the neck and create a balanced look, enhancing the bust area without overwhelming it.

   - **Try This**: Wrap dresses and tops with V-necklines that flatter your upper body while highlighting your waist.

   3. **Choose Straight-Leg or Bootcut Pants**
   - **Why**: Straight-leg or bootcut pants maintain the balance between your hips and lower body, lengthening the legs and complementing your curves.

   - **Try This**: Pair high-waisted, straight-leg pants with a tucked-in blouse or a fitted top to create a smooth, flattering line.

4. **Highlight with Wrap Dresses**
   - ○ **Why**: Wrap dresses are a classic choice for Hourglass shapes, pulling in at the waist and creating a beautiful, balanced silhouette.

   - ○ **Try This**: Choose a wrap dress in a solid colour or a subtle print for an elegant, timeless look that emphasises your natural proportions.

Current Trends for Dressing Hourglass Body Shapes

Who doesn't love a little trend play? With an Hourglass body shape, you have a lot of freedom to experiment with modern styles while still staying true to what flatters your figure. Here's how to rock some of today's biggest trends:

1. **Bodycon Dresses and Pencil Skirts**
   - ○ **Why**: Bodycon dresses and pencil skirts hug your curves and emphasise your waist, creating a sleek, confident silhouette.

   - ○ **Try This**: Look for bodycon dresses in soft, stretchy fabrics that allow you to move comfortably. A high-waisted pencil skirt paired with a tucked-in blouse or crop top is another fabulous option.

2. **High-Waisted, Flared Jeans**
   - ○ **Why**: High-waisted flares are not only trendy, but they also emphasise the waist and elongate the legs, balancing your proportions.

   - ○ **Try This**: Pair high-waisted flared jeans with a fitted blouse or cropped sweater for a fun, retro-inspired look that highlights your figure.

3. **Belted Blazers and Outerwear**
   - ○ **Why**: Blazers and jackets with belts are on-trend and ideal for the hourglass body shape, as they define the waist and enhance the overall silhouette.

- **Try This**: Choose tailored blazers with a waist belt or cinched design to create an elegant, polished look that works for both office and evening wear.

4. **Corset and Bustier Tops**
   - **Why**: Corset-style tops and bustiers are making a comeback, and they're fantastic for Hourglass figures as they accentuate the waist and highlight the bust.

   - **Try This**: Pair a corset top with high-waisted pants or a fitted skirt to create a modern, daring look that enhances your natural body shape.

5. **Asymmetrical Cuts and Slits**
   - **Why**: Asymmetrical hemlines and high slits create visual interest, adding an edgy touch to your look while enhancing your curves.

   - **Try This**: Dresses or skirts with asymmetrical hems and thigh-high slits bring a fun, contemporary vibe to your wardrobe without compromising on elegance.

Before & After Styling Exercises

Here are some examples showing the transformative power of dressing to flatter your Hourglass body shape. Small adjustments in fit, structure, and styling can have a big impact:

1. **From Boxy to Beautifully Balanced**: See the difference between an oversized, loose top and a fitted, waist-defining blouse. Defining the waist makes the look feel polished and balanced.

2. **From Shapeless to Curvaceous**: Notice how a boxy dress changes dramatically when swapped for a body-hugging wrap dress that emphasises your curves.

3. **From Unstructured to Streamlined**: Compare a pair of low-rise pants with high-waisted, straight-leg jeans. The higher waist defines the body shape, creating a streamlined, elongated look.

Share Your Journey with Us

Share your experience with us to help guide other Hourglass body-shaped readers. Head to stylebyaudra.com and sign up for a free membership, which will enable you to join our community, build a style profile and share your journey with us! You will also be the first to know of any updates, brand collaborations and styling workshops coming to a city near you. Let's make our learning fun and interactive! You will also be the first to know of any updates, brand collaborations and styling workshops coming to a city near you. Let's make our learning fun and interactive!

Embracing Your Body Shape

As an Hourglass Body Shape, you have the flexibility to try many different styles, from fitted dresses to high-waisted pants and belted jackets. Your silhouette is naturally balanced, giving you the freedom to experiment while still creating harmony. Don't be afraid to embrace fitted silhouettes that showcase your curves. You're built for them!

Remember, style is all about expression, and dressing for your body shape is about enhancing what you already have. Whether you're aiming for elegance, casual cool, or a little glamour, there are endless ways to create outfits that reflect your unique beauty. Your hourglass figure is a gift. Celebrate it with every outfit you choose!

Visual Inspiration Gallery

Explore a variety of looks designed for Hourglass shapes. From belted dresses to high-waisted tailoring, these visuals highlight your natural curves and showcase styles that accentuate the waist while maintaining balance. Use these ideas to create a wardrobe that embraces your proportions and empowers your style. Reference: Outfit Layout (Top to Bottom, Left to Right).

• Look #1: Refined Contrast and Curve

A fitted ivory blouse is tucked into a slate blue high-waisted pencil skirt, layered under a soft rose tailored coat. This structured ensemble showcases the waist and highlights the hourglass silhouette with timeless elegance.

• Look #2: Depth and Dimension in Neutrals

A rich teal turtleneck tucked into high-waisted wide-leg trousers anchors this deep grey double-breasted coat. The cinched waist and soft draping balance the frame while elongating the legs, giving a refined and powerful look for colder seasons.

• Look #3: Casual Harmony in Soft Blue

A sleeveless powder-blue romper cinched at the waist is paired with a light beige blazer. This outfit defines the waist and elongates the legs while offering a relaxed but refined silhouette.

• Look #4: Textured Elegance with Wrap Detailing

A cream-toned mini wrap dress with a deep V-neckline hugs the curves and defines the waist. The hourglass figure is elevated with soft draping and pointed pumps, balanced with a structured tote for polish.

Figure 13

Figure 14

Figure 15

Figure 16

Hourglass Body Shape Style Tips

- **Go-To Outfit Formula**: Wrap dress or belted blazer + fitted pencil skirt or tailored pants.

- **Key Tips**: Emphasise the waist and show off balanced curves with fitted pieces that hug the body.

- **Essential Fabrics**: Stretch fabrics and soft knits that define curves and create smooth lines. For more subtlety, use structured fabrics such as cotton and linen.

Ready for the Next Body shape?

Feel free to revisit these tips whenever you're looking to refine your look. This book has styling advice for every body shape, so if you're curious about how different silhouettes are styled, keep exploring. Each chapter is filled with possibilities that celebrate all types of beauty.

Now, let's move on to the next chapter, where we'll dive into the style secrets for athletic body shape and discover how to add dimension, body shape, and personality to every outfit!

Chapter 5: Dressing for Athletic Body Shapes

If you've got similar measurements across your shoulders, waist, and hips, then you have what's often called an "athletic" or "straight" body shape. Your figure offers amazing versatility. Think Cameron Diaz, Natalie Portman, and Gwyneth Paltrow, who all showcase the Athletic body shape's stylish possibilities. You have a naturally balanced silhouette that's perfect for experimenting with lines, layers, and textures to create curves, add dimension, and play with proportions.

In this chapter, we'll explore timeless styling tips and some of today's trendiest looks to show off your body shape in a way that feels both empowering and fun. Let's dive into the world of styling for Athletic body shapes and discover how to make every outfit feel fresh and fabulous!

Understanding the Athletic Body Shape

The Athletic body shape, also known as the rectangle or column body shape, is known for its balanced, streamlined silhouette. Key characteristics include:

- **Even Measurements**: Your shoulders, waist, and hips are similar in width, giving you a naturally balanced look.

- **Straight Waistline**: Unlike other shapes, your waist is less defined, creating a clean, straight silhouette.

- **Lean Proportions**: Many ladies with Athletic body shapes have a naturally lean, athletic build, with fewer curves but lots of versatility in styling.

Athletic body shapes look amazing in outfits that add definition to the waist, create curves, and add volume to different areas. With the right cuts and combinations, you can easily add form and dimension to your look, making your wardrobe feel fun, dynamic, and perfectly suited to your style.

Classic Tips for Dressing Athletic Body Shapes

These tried-and-true styling principles will help you bring unique shape and balance to your silhouette, creating outfits that make the most of your naturally balanced figure.

1. **Create Curves with Belts and Waist-Defining Styles**
   - **Why**: Adding definition at the waist creates the illusion of curves and helps balance the upper and lower body.

   - **Try This**: Look for dresses with belts, high-waisted pants, or wrap dresses that pull in at the waist. Adding a belt to any outfit can instantly bring structure and body shape.

2. **Add Volume to the Upper or Lower Body**
   - **Why**: Adding volume in one area, like the shoulders or hips, creates contrast and enhances your body shape.

   - **Try This**: Try tops with puff sleeves, ruffles, or embellishments, or opt for skirts with a bit of flair. These details add visual interest and create the illusion of curves.

3. **Play with Layering and Textures**
   - **Why**: Layering and different textures create depth, adding dimension to a more streamlined silhouette.

   - **Try This**: Belted cardigans, structured blazers, and layered tops are all great choices for athletic body shapes. Look for pieces with interesting fabrics like knits, tweed, or leather to add texture.

4. **Choose A-Line and Flared Skirts**
   - **Why**: A-line and flared skirts create a feminine silhouette by adding form around the hips.

- **Try This**: A-line skirts or flared dresses that accentuate the waist and flow out from the hips. This classic look works beautifully for creating balance and body shape.

5. **Contrast Tops and Bottoms**
   - **Why**: This adds interest and definition and accentuates an athletic body shape.
   - **Try This**: Contrast a loose or flowy pair of pants with a more structured top, or a ruffled top with a pair of tailored pants.

Current Trends for Dressing Athletic Body Shapes

Fashion trends are filled with creative opportunities for athletic body shapes. With a naturally balanced figure, you can play with volume, patterns, and layering to create fresh, eye-catching looks. Let's explore some of today's hottest trends and how they work for your body shape.

1. **Statement Belts and Corset Tops**
   - **Why**: Statement belts and corset-inspired tops emphasise the waist and add definition to your figure.

   - **Try This**: Pair a fitted corset top with high-waisted pants or add a bold belt to a relaxed dress. These pieces add a dramatic twist to your look while accentuating the waist.

2. **Oversized Blazers and Jackets**
   - **Why**: Oversized outerwear is a big trend and works perfectly for athletic body shapes by adding volume to the shoulders and hips, balancing out a straight silhouette.

   - **Try This**: Wear an oversized blazer over a fitted top with jeans, or try a boyfriend-style jacket with a belted waist to create form and structure.

3. **Layered Looks with Cropped Tops**
   o **Why**: Cropped tops paired with high-waisted bottoms visually shorten the torso and define the waist, adding curves to a straight body shape.

   o **Try This**: Try layering a cropped sweater over a fitted tee and high-waisted pants, or wear a cropped jacket over a dress to create a curvier look.

4. **Ruching and Draped Fabrics**
   o **Why**: Ruching and draped fabrics create the appearance of curves and add dimension to the body.
   o **Try This**: Dresses or skirts with ruching at the hips or bust can help create form and highlight your silhouette. Draped blouses also add softness and curves to a streamlined figure.

5. **Bold Prints and Patterns**
   o **Why**: Eye-catching prints and patterns add volume and draw attention to different areas, creating contrast and depth.

   o **Try This**: Choose tops or bottoms with bold stripes, florals, or geometric patterns and contrast with plainer pieces to break up the straight lines and add a fun, modern twist to your look.

Before & After Styling Exercises

Sometimes, subtle tweaks can make a big impact on your overall look. Here are a few before-and-after examples to show how small adjustments can transform an outfit:

1. **From Straight to Curved**: See the difference between an unbelted dress and one with a bold belt that defines the waist and adds curves.

2. **From Flat to Dimensional**: Compare how a loose top looks next to a layered outfit with a fitted top and a puff-sleeve jacket. Layering and volume add depth and body shape.

3. **From Simple to Stylish**: Notice how swapping plain pants for high-waisted, wide-leg trousers creates a more balanced, sophisticated look by emphasising the waist and adding volume.

Share Your Journey with Us

Share your experience with us to help guide other Athletic body-shaped readers. Head to stylebyaudra.com and sign up for a free membership, which will enable you to join our community, build a style profile and share your journey with us! You will also be the first to know of any updates, brand collaborations and styling workshops coming to a city near you. Let's make our learning fun and interactive! You will also be the first to know of any updates, brand collaborations and styling workshops coming to a city near you. Let's make our learning fun and interactive!

Embracing Your Body Shape

With your athletic body shape, you're like a blank canvas with endless styling possibilities! You can effortlessly pull off tailored looks, play with volume, or add structure to create a balanced, sophisticated look. Dressing for your body shape is all about enhancing what you already have, whether it's defining your waist, creating curves, or adding texture.

Remember, your unique shape offers incredible versatility, allowing you to experiment with different looks and find a style that feels true to who you are. Whether you're heading to the office, meeting friends, or enjoying a night out, your wardrobe can reflect your confidence, creativity, and individuality.

Visual Inspiration Gallery

Explore a variety of looks designed for Athletic body shapes. With balanced proportions and a naturally straight silhouette, these outfits are crafted to add curves, enhance dimension, and define the waist. Each look shows how to play with texture, contrast and layering to create a more dynamic frame. Reference: Outfit Layout (Top to Bottom, Left to Right)

• **Look #1: Streamlined Texture with Waist Focus**

A fitted ivory turtleneck crop top is paired with a high-waisted emerald pleated skirt. The vertical pleats add movement, and the belt draws attention to the waist, while tall cognac boots bring elegance and visual lift to the legs, perfect for building shape on an athletic silhouette.

• **Look #2: Sorbet Layers and Tailored Lines**

A soft mint overcoat frames a vanilla peplum blouse tucked into high-waisted tan trousers. The structured outerwear adds volume, while the subtle flare of the peplum defines the waist. A pink handbag softens the palette and balances this crisp, colour-blocked ensemble.

• **Look #3: Smart Shorts with Pop of Colour**

This breezy summer look features a lime green sleeveless top tucked into high-waisted beige shorts, layered with a soft ivory blazer. The bold pop of colour adds interest to the upper body, while the cinched waist and textural layering give curves to an otherwise straight figure.

• **Look #4: Knit Drama and Belted Definition**

A rich plum knit dress is cinched with a nude belt and layered under a deep navy oversized coat. The high neckline adds sophistication while the belt creates shape. Nude boots elongate the legs and bring balance, making this an ideal choice for colder days that still highlight the waistline.

Figure 17

Figure 18

Figure 19

Figure 20

Athletic Body Shape Style Tips

- **Go-To Outfit Formula**: Layered or textured top + high-waisted, flared jeans or an A-line skirt.

- **Key Tips**: Add volume and form with textured fabrics, patterns, and layers that bring depth to your look.

- **Essential Fabrics**: Structured or textured fabrics like linen and tweed to create dimension.

Ready for the Next Body shape?

Return to these tips whenever you need a little styling refresh. This book has styling secrets for every body type, so if you're curious about other shapes or just want to explore, keep reading!

Let's keep the momentum going and move on to Chapter 6, where we'll explore all the best styling options for the strawberry body shape. Get ready for more fun, fashion, and tips tailored just for you!

Chapter 6: Dressing for Strawberry Body Shapes

If your shoulders are broader than your hips and you have a naturally structured silhouette, welcome to your perfect style guide. Celebrities like Angelina Jolie, Naomi Campbell, and Charlize Theron share your body shape, showing how beautifully the Strawberry body shape silhouette can carry fashion's boldest looks. With a bit of styling finesse, you can create gorgeous balance, highlight your best features, and embrace your unique body shape with confidence.

In this chapter, we'll explore classic styling tips and the latest trends that bring harmony and elegance to the strawberry body shape. Let's celebrate your strong upper body and dive into looks that are balanced, stylish, and totally you!

Understanding the Strawberry Body Shape

The strawberry body shape is known for its broad shoulders and narrower lower body. Key features include:

- **Broad Shoulders**: Your shoulders are often the widest part of your frame, giving you a striking, confident silhouette.
- **Narrower Hips**: Compared to your shoulders, your hips and thighs are slimmer, creating a lovely taper.
- **Defined Waist**: Your waist is usually more defined than an apple body shape and an athletically shaped body, which gives you the flexibility to experiment with waist-defining styles.

With your bold shoulders and elegant body shape, you look fabulous in outfits that bring attention downward, add volume to the lower section of your body, and create balance with the upper body. The goal here is to enhance your natural silhouette while experimenting with layers, lines, and cuts that bring harmony to your look.

Classic Tips for Dressing Strawberry Shapes

These timeless tips will help you create a balanced silhouette, drawing attention to your lower body and adding beautiful curves. With these foundational styles, you'll feel polished and confident.

1. **Draw Attention to the Lower Body**
   - **Why**: Adding volume and visual interest to the lower body helps balance the broader shoulders, creating an overall harmonious look.

   - **Try This**: Go for skirts with ruffles, pleats, or A-line cuts. A-line skirts or wide-leg pants add fullness to the hips and create a softer, balanced silhouette.

2. **Choose V-Necks and Scoop Necks**
   - **Why**: V-necks and scoop necks break up the width of the shoulders, creating a more streamlined look and drawing the eye vertically.

   - **Try This**: Look for V-neck blouses, wrap tops, and scoop-neck dresses. These necklines are flattering and add elegance without widening the upper body.

3. **Opt for Darker Colours on Top**
   - **Why**: Darker shades on the upper body visually minimize the shoulders, while lighter shades on the lower body create contrast and balance.

   - **Try This**: Choose darker tops paired with lighter or patterned skirts and pants. This contrast keeps the focus on the lower body and creates a beautifully proportioned look.

4. **Go for A-Line and Flared Skirts**
   - **Why**: A-line and flared skirts bring volume to the hips, helping balance broader shoulders and creating an hourglass body shape.

- **Try This**: Midi or maxi A-line skirts in bright colours, patterns, or textures are fabulous choices that add movement and balance to your look.

5. **Balance with Soft, Flowing Fabrics**
   - **Why**: Soft, flowing fabrics on the upper body soften the shoulders, creating a gentler line that balances the overall silhouette.

   - **Try This**: Look for blouses with light draping or soft materials like silk and chiffon. Pair them with structured bottoms for a balanced, refined style.

Current Trends for Dressing Strawberry Body Shapes

Fashion trends are full of fresh ideas for strawberry shapes, allowing you to experiment with fun, modern looks while keeping balance in mind. Let's explore some of today's hottest styles that work beautifully for your silhouette.

1. **Statement Skirts and Bold Printed Bottoms**
   - **Why**: Bold prints, bright colours, and unique details on the lower body draw attention away from the shoulders and bring balance.

   - **Try This**: Choose patterned midi skirts or wide-leg pants in vibrant hues to create interest and add volume below the waistline.

2. **High-Waisted Wide-Leg Pants**
   - **Why**: High-waisted, wide-leg pants add fullness to the hips and thighs, creating a curvier look that balances your body shape.

   - **Try This**: Pair high-waisted pants in a light or patterned fabric with a tucked-in, fitted blouse for a chic, balanced look.

3. **One-shoulder and Asymmetrical Necklines**
   - **Why**: Asymmetrical necklines add an interesting twist to your look, breaking up the width of the shoulders and creating a unique visual effect.

o **Try This**: Try one-shoulder tops or asymmetrical blouses to add flair to your look while drawing attention upward in a balanced way.

4. **Soft, Oversized Cardigans and Wrap Coats**
   o **Why**: Soft outerwear layers create a relaxed look, softening the shoulder line and adding dimension.

   o **Try This**: Pair a long, flowy cardigan with a fitted top and wide-leg pants for a cozy, balanced outfit. Wrap coats with waist ties are also a great choice for adding definition without bulk.

5. **Tiered and Ruffled Skirts**
   o **Why**: Ruffles and tiers add volume and movement to the lower body, creating a balanced, feminine silhouette.

   o **Try This**: Tiered midi skirts or ruffled miniskirts in playful prints or textures create a fun, trendy look that draws attention to your lower body.

Before & After Styling Exercises

Small adjustments can make a big difference in bringing balance to the strawberry body shape. Here are a few examples to show how subtle styling tweaks can transform an outfit:

1. **From Top-Heavy to Balanced**: See the impact of switching from a fitted, plain skirt to a tiered, patterned skirt that draws attention downward and balances the upper body.

2. **From Broad to Softly Streamlined**: Notice how replacing a straight-across neckline with a V-neck softens the shoulders and creates a visually elongated line.

3. **From Plain to Playful**: Compare a basic top with a one-shoulder blouse that adds a fun, modern twist while maintaining balance.

Share Your Journey with Us

Share your experience with us to help guide other Strawberry body-shaped readers. Head to stylebyaudra.com and sign up for a free membership, which will enable you to join our community, build a style profile and share your journey with us! You will also be the first to know of any updates, brand collaborations and styling workshops coming to a city near you. Let's make our learning fun and interactive!

Embracing Your Body Shape

The strawberry body shape is all about strength and elegance. With broad shoulders that add a natural sense of poise and presence, you can carry off a range of styles beautifully. Dressing for your body shape is about celebrating what makes you unique and experimenting with proportions to achieve balance and harmony.

Whether you're heading to a meeting, a night out, or a casual brunch, remember that dressing for your unique body shape offers endless possibilities. Style is a journey, and as you play with textures, colours, and silhouettes, you're creating a wardrobe that reflects your confidence and personality.

Visual Inspiration Gallery

Explore a curated selection of looks designed for the Strawberry body shapes. These outfits balance broader shoulders by drawing the eye downward, creating harmony with volume and colour in the lower half. From structured coats to playful skirts, each look embraces bold proportions while offering visual softness. Reference: Outfit Layout (Top to Bottom, Left to Right)

• Look #1: Soft Power in Colour Blocking

A deep green fitted top paired with a high-waisted blush mini skirt immediately brings focus to the legs. The long rose overcoat softens the shoulder line, while black over-the-knee boots anchor the outfit and add visual length to the lower body.

- **Look #2: Monochrome Simplicity with Balance**

This black V-neck blouse with rolled sleeves keeps the upper body sleek, allowing the high-waisted houndstooth shorts to take centre stage. The subtle print and added volume below help balance the broader shoulder line with effortless chic.

- **Look #3: Navy-on-Navy Structured Fluidity**

A classic wide-leg navy pantsuit is paired with a long navy coat, creating vertical balance and elongation. The deep tones and flowy silhouette soften the upper body and add visual volume to the lower half—ideal for strawberry shapes craving structure and movement.

- **Look #4: Luxe Layers and Vibrant Contrast**

A berry-toned blouse and magenta mini skirt create a striking lower-body focus under a rich chocolate trench coat. The shiny texture and bold colour block bring drama to the bottom half, while the collar and coat streamline the upper silhouette with polish.

Strawberry Body Shape Style Tips

- o **Go-To Outfit Formula**: Dark, tailored top + patterned or ruffled skirt or wide-leg pants.

- o **Key Tips**: Soften the upper body with simple cuts and draw attention to the hips with volume or bold prints on the lower section of your body.

- o **Essential Fabrics**: Loose fabrics on top and structured or textured materials on the lower body.

Next: Understanding Fabrics, Patterns, and Colours

Now that you've explored the best cuts, silhouettes, and outfit combinations for your unique body shape, it's time to enhance your styling knowledge with the secret ingredients that can take your wardrobe from good to great: fabric, pattern, and colour. In the next chapter, we'll dive into how different fabrics behave on different silhouettes, how patterns can shape perception and balance, and how colour placement, when done with right, can amplify or soften your natural proportions. Think of it as the artistic palette behind the masterpiece that is your wardrobe.

Chapter 7: The Role of Fabrics, Patterns, and Colours

Welcome to one of the most exciting parts of styling: exploring the world of fabrics, patterns, and colours! These elements are the building blocks of every outfit, and when chosen thoughtfully, they can completely transform how clothing enhances your unique body shape. Just as the right colours and prints can bring a look to life, the right fabrics can create movement, structure, and a polished finish.

This chapter will walk you through how to select the best fabrics, patterns, and colours to flatter each body shape, helping you create a wardrobe that feels as good as it looks.

Fabric Choices for Each Body Shape

When it comes to fabric, everybody's shape benefits from different textures, draping, and structure. Here's how to pick fabrics that will work in harmony with your body type, creating a look that feels tailored to you.

1. **Apple Body Shape**
   - **Best Fabrics**: Lightweight fabrics that drape gracefully without clinging, like silk, satin, and soft knits, work wonders for apple body shapes. These fabrics create smooth lines and draw attention downward, balancing the broader shoulders.

   - **Avoid**: Bulky fabrics like thick wool or heavy knits on top, which can add volume to the upper body.

   - **Try This**: A silk blouse paired with structured, high-waisted pants. The softness of the silk balances broader shoulders, while the tailored pants create the definition below.

2. **Pear Body Shape**
   - o **Best Fabrics**: Structured fabrics for bottoms (like denim, twill, and wool) paired with lighter, more detailed fabrics on top (like chiffon, lace, or satin). This contrast adds volume to the upper body while enhancing the natural form of the hips.

   - o **Avoid**: Shiny or clingy fabrics on the lower body, as they can add unnecessary emphasis to the hips.

   - o **Try This**: A lightweight, patterned blouse with a fitted pair of high-waisted jeans. The soft top adds volume and interest to the upper body, while the jeans hug the hips in a flattering way.

3. **Hourglass Body Shape**
   - o **Best Fabrics**: Fabrics that contour the body without being too tight are ideal for hourglass body shapes. Think stretch cotton, jersey, and soft knits. These fabrics enhance natural curves, moving with your body and defining the waist.

   - o **Avoid**: Stiff or boxy fabrics, which can hide your curves or create bulk where it's not needed.

   - o **Try This**: A fitted jersey wrap dress that highlights the waist and drapes naturally over your curves. This fabric provides a streamlined, polished look while showing off your body shape.

4. **Athletic Body Shape**
   - o **Best Fabrics**: Textured fabrics, such as linen, tweed, and ribbed knits, add dimension and depth to an athletic body shape. These fabrics create a curvier look, adding form without clinging.

- Avoid: Thin, clingy fabrics, which can emphasize a straight silhouette instead of adding body shape.

- Try This: A linen blouse with pleats paired with wide-leg trousers in a similar texture. The linen adds structure, while pleats create curves and add movement to your look.

5. **Strawberry Body Shape**
   - Best Fabrics: Flowing fabrics like chiffon, silk, and lightweight cotton work beautifully on the upper body. Pair them with structured fabrics on the lower section of your body, like denim or tailored wool, to add volume to the hips.

   - Avoid: Stiff or heavy fabrics on top, which can accentuate the shoulders.
   - Try This: A soft chiffon blouse tucked into a pair of structured, wide-leg trousers. The flowing blouse softens the shoulders, while the structured pants add form to the lower section of your body.

Explore Patterns and Prints

Patterns are one of the best ways to express personal style while also creating balance, enhancing body shape, and adding energy to an outfit. The expert skill is in knowing how to place patterns so that they work in harmony with your body shape

1. **Apple Body Shape**
   - Best Patterns: Patterns that bring focus to the lower body are ideal for apple body shapes, as they balance broader shoulders. Vertical stripes, subtle florals, and dark, solid tops with printed skirts or pants work beautifully.

   - Try This: Pair a dark, solid blouse with a skirt featuring a subtle floral or geometric pattern. This draws attention to the lower section of your body and creates a sense of balance.

2. **Pear Body Shape**
   - ○ **Best Patterns**: Use bold patterns on top to add interest and volume to the upper body. Horizontal stripes, plaids, and eye-catching prints are great choices. Keep the lower body in solid or darker colours to create balance.

   - ○ **Try This**: Wear a striped, puff-sleeve blouse with dark, fitted pants. The stripes add width to the shoulders, creating an Hourglass effect.

3. **Hourglass Body Shape**
   - ○ **Best Patterns**: Hourglass body shapes look fantastic in evenly distributed patterns, as they emphasize balanced proportions. Small to medium-sized prints, polka dots, and delicate florals that don't overwhelm the framework well.

   - ○ **Try This**: A wrap dress with a small, even floral print enhances your natural silhouette by creating a streamlined silhouette that complements your curves.

4. **Athletic Body Shape**
   - ○ **Best Patterns**: Patterns that create the illusion of curves, like diagonal stripes, chevrons, and large florals, add depth and dimension to an athletic body shape.
   - ○ **Try This**: A fitted blouse with diagonal stripes paired with an A-line skirt in a solid colour. The diagonal lines create a sense of body shape, while the A-line skirt adds volume at the hips.

5. **Strawberry Body Shape**
   - ○ **Best Patterns**: Use patterns on the lower body to add fullness and balance broader shoulders. Polka dots, wide stripes, and playful prints work well on skirts and pants.

- **Try This**: Wear a solid, dark-coloured top with a polka-dot midi skirt. The dots add volume to the hips, creating a balanced look.

Choosing Right: Best Colours for Your Body Shape

Colour can be transformative when it comes to styling for body types. Light, dark, warm, or cool tones each have their own effect, and strategic use of colour can highlight or downplay different areas. Selecting the right colours for your wardrobe can enhance your natural features, complement your body shape, and elevate your overall style. This section will guide you through understanding how to align colours with your unique skin tone while maintaining a balance with your body type.

Identify Your Skin Undertone: Skin tones fall into three categories. Warm, cool, and neutral:

- **Warm undertones**: Your skin has golden or yellowish hues. Think earthy tones like olive green, coral, mustard, and gold—they'll make you glow!

- **Cool undertones**: You've got pink or bluish hues in your skin. Jewel tones like emerald, green, sapphire blue, and fuchsia are your best friends.

- **Neutral undertones**: Lucky you! You can wear most colours, but soft pastels or muted tones like taupe or dusty pink look especially lovely on you.

Apply Colour Principles to Body Shapes

Apple Body Shapes: Choose darker colours or monochromatic schemes for the upper body to create a slimming effect, paired with brighter or patterned colours on the lower body to draw attention to your legs.

- **Best Colours**: Darker tones on top (like navy, charcoal, or deep jewel tones) with lighter or brighter colours on the bottom help balance an apple body shape.

- **Try This**: Pair a navy blouse with a bright-coloured skirt or pants. This combination draws attention to the lower body and balances the silhouette.

- **Pear Body Shapes**: Focus on vibrant or embellished tops to highlight the upper body and balance wider hips. Muted or darker tones on the lower body can minimize attention.

- **Best Colours**: Light or bright colours on top and darker shades on the bottom create a balanced look, emphasizing the upper body and minimizing the hips.

- **Try This**: Wear a soft pastel blouse with dark-wash jeans or trousers. This pairing highlights the upper body, creating a balanced look.

Hourglass Body Shapes: Emphasize curves with balanced colour placement. Use form-fitting clothes in bold hues that don't overshadow the natural body shape.

- **Best Colours**: Monochromatic or evenly distributed colours are great for Hourglass shapes, as they enhance natural balance and harmony.

- **Try This**: A fitted dress in a single, bold colour emphasizes your curves and creates a cohesive look. Deep jewel tones or rich neutrals are perfect choices.

Athletic Body Shapes: Create visual curves with contrasting colours and patterns at the waist or hips.

- **Best Colours**: Colour-blocking or contrasting colours help create the illusion of curves and add dimension. Combining bright tops with darker bottoms (or vice versa) creates visual interest.

- **Try This**: Try a colour-blocked dress or pairing a bright top with dark pants to add contrast and body shape.

Strawberry Shapes: Highlight the lower body with vibrant colours or prints, keeping the top section of your body streamlined in softer shades to balance broad shoulders.

- **Best Colours**: Dark colours on top with lighter shades or bold patterns on the lower body create balance by drawing the eye downward.

- **Try This**: Wear a dark, fitted blouse with light-coloured wide-leg trousers. This combination keeps the upper body sleek and adds volume to the lower section of your body.

Bringing it All Together

Choosing fabrics, patterns, and colours with intention can turn your wardrobe into a curated collection that feels perfect for *you*. By combining the right textures, patterns, and hues, you can enhance your natural body shape, create visual harmony, and bring out your best features in every outfit.

Whether you're drawn to the elegance of silk, the structure of tweed, the fun of florals, or the richness of jewel tones, remember that every choice is an opportunity to express yourself. Fabrics, patterns, and colours are here to work with you, elevating your style and giving you the confidence to shine.

Visual Inspiration Gallery:

Below are examples of fabric, pattern, and colour combinations crafted for each body type. These visuals show how strategic fabric placement can flatter each silhouette, whether by elongating the body, highlighting the waist, or drawing attention to your best features.

Bringing it All Together

Choosing fabrics, patterns, and colours with intention can turn your wardrobe into a curated collection that feels perfect for *you*. By combining the right textures, patterns, and hues, you can enhance your natural body shape, create visual harmony, and bring out your best features in every outfit.

Whether you're drawn to the elegance of silk, the structure of tweed, the fun of florals, or the richness of jewel tones, remember that every choice is an opportunity to express yourself. Fabrics, patterns, and colours are here to work with you, elevating your style and giving you the confidence to shine.

Visual Inspiration Gallery:

Below are examples of fabric, pattern, and colour combinations crafted for each body type. These visuals show how strategic fabric placement can flatter each silhouette, whether by elongating the body, highlighting the waist, or drawing attention to your best features.

Apple Body Shape Ideal Fabric Placement Examples:

Figure 25

Figure 26

Apple Body Shape – Ideal Fabric Placement Examples

• **Look #1:** A navy pinstripe blazer over a deep green blouse and matching high-waisted trousers elongates the torso and draws the eye downward. The vertical pattern adds structure and a slimming effect, while the darker tones balance the broader upper body.

• **Look #2:** A soft grey wrap top paired with a voluminous ivory floral skirt provides contrast in both texture and colour. The full skirt adds balance to the upper body, while the floral print brings attention to the lower half.

Pear Body Shape Ideal Fabric Placement Examples:

Figure 27

Figure 28

Pear Body Shape – Ideal Fabric Placement Examples

• **Look #1:** A vibrant plaid shirt with puffed sleeves adds volume and dimension to the upper body. Balanced with sleek black wide-leg trousers, this look draws the eye upward while softening the hip area.

• **Look #2:** A soft cream blouse tucked into dark skinny jeans features vertical seam detailing that elongates the legs. The light top pulls visual weight upward, balancing the fuller hips.

Hourglass Body Shape Ideal Fabric Placement Examples:

Figure 29

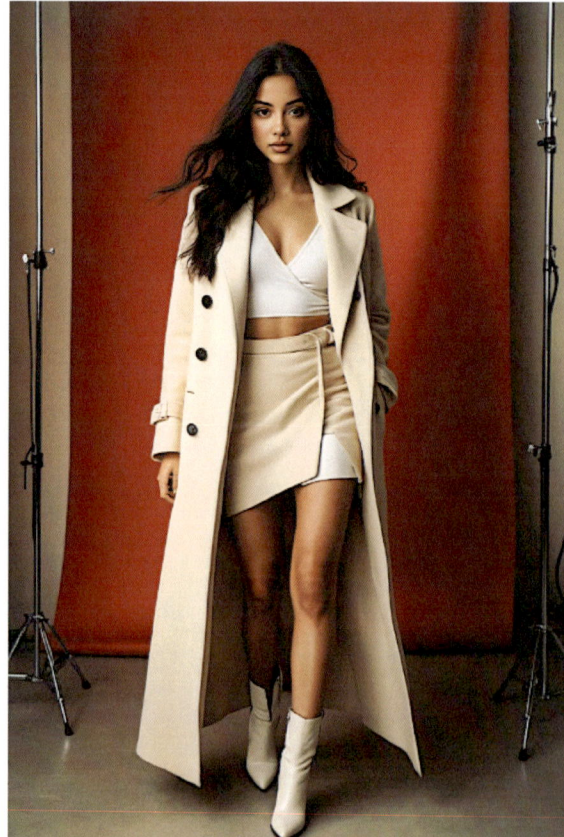

Figure 30

Hourglass Body Shape – Ideal Fabric Placement Examples

• **Look #1:** A beige wrap dress with subtle texture hugs the waist and enhances natural curves. The soft neutral colour keeps the focus on body shape rather than bold pattern, creating elegant balance.

• **Look #2:** A structured cream coat layered over a matching crop and skirt set showcases harmony in fit and fabric. The ensemble highlights the waist while maintaining symmetry at the shoulders and hips.

Athletic Body Shape Ideal Fabric Placement Examples:

Figure 31

Figure 32

Athletic Body Shape – Ideal Fabric Placement Examples

• **Look #1:** Statement floral trousers introduce volume and print to the lower body, while a dark bandeau top keeps the upper silhouette minimal. This contrast builds the illusion of curves and adds interest.

• **Look #2:** A belted cream shirt dress adds soft draping and waist definition to a straight frame. The structured shoulders paired with a cinched waist create body shape and visual interest.

Strawberry Body Shape Ideal Fabric Placement Examples:

Figure 33

Figure 34

Strawberry Body Shape – Ideal Fabric Placement Examples

• **Look #1:** A dark, simple V-neck top paired with a flowy, tiered pink skirt redirects the eye downward and adds softness to the hips, balancing broader shoulders beautifully.

• **Look #2:** A tucked-in navy blouse with striped wide-leg pants elongates the lower body while keeping the upper body streamlined. The vertical lines and light fabric on the bottom shift attention and create proportional elegance.

Ready to Build Your Dream Wardrobe?

With your new insights into fabrics, patterns, and colours, you're well on your way to creating a wardrobe that's not only stylish but also tailored to you. Up next is Chapter 8, where you'll discover how you can build a capsule wardrobe that is just right for you. Find curated fashion pieces for your unique body shape and wardrobe accessories on our online store! Celebrate your unique style with handy tools from our brand that help you remember all that you have learned about your body shape! Let's discover how to build a stunning capsule wardrobe and maintain style balance and fashion confidence, with our capsule wardrobe guide! Visit audraoakes.com.au for more resources and handy tools for organising your wardrobe.

Chapter 8: Capsule Wardrobe, Tailored to You

Welcome to the chapter where we bring it all together! You've learned how to dress for your unique body type, whether that's an Apple Body Shape, Pear Body Shape, Hourglass Body Shape, Athletic Body Shape, or Strawberry Body Shape. Now, we're going to take things a step further by creating a capsule wardrobe that's tailored to your body shape, packed with pieces that make styling effortless, and that works beautifully from season to season.

A capsule wardrobe is a curated collection of essential pieces that you can mix, match, and style in endless ways. It's all about simplicity, versatility, and quality over quantity, perfect for those who want a stress-free way to get dressed. Let's dive into the essentials of building a capsule wardrobe that's timeless, body-type-friendly, and, above all, fun to wear!

What is a Capsule Wardrobe?

The idea of a capsule wardrobe is simple: instead of a closet overflowing with clothes, you pare down to a selection of versatile, high-quality essentials that you love. Think of it as a wardrobe *'greatest hits'* collection, with pieces that are easy to mix and match to create a wide variety of looks. A well-designed capsule wardrobe saves time, simplifies your life, and lets you focus on wearing what makes you feel fabulous every day.

A capsule wardrobe is more than just a minimalist trend. It's a way to create a wardrobe that reflects your true self. Every time you open your closet, you'll find pieces that fit, flatter, and make you feel confident. Whether you're dressing up for work, a date, or a casual weekend, your capsule wardrobe will help you look and feel fantastic with ease. So, take your time, enjoy the process, and let your capsule wardrobe be a celebration of your unique body shape, style, and spirit!

Whether you're going for a more minimalist wardrobe or simply looking to streamline your options, a capsule wardrobe is a game-changer.

And when tailored to your body type, it becomes a wardrobe that works *with* you, helping you look your best effortlessly.

My Capsule Wardrobe Content Philosophy

A truly functional wardrobe is more than a collection of clothes. It is a carefully curated toolkit that serves your lifestyle, expresses your personality, and stands the test of time. Drawing on timeless styling principles and the guidance of leading fashion institutes such as the Fashion Institute of Technology (FIT) and the London College of Fashion, my philosophy is rooted in both versatility and individuality.

60% Minimalist Clothing Style

The foundation of a well-curated wardrobe should consist of around 60% minimalist, timeless pieces. These are classic, neutral-toned garments, think tailored trousers, crisp button-down shirts, well-fitted jeans, neutral knitwear, and simple dresses, that can be easily mixed and matched. According to industry styling experts, a strong foundation of basics reduces decision fatigue, makes daily dressing more efficient, and ensures you always have something appropriate to wear for any occasion. In the context of this book, these pieces form the 'canvas' for your body shape–specific styling.

30% Trend-Forward Pieces

The next 30% of your wardrobe should reflect current trends and seasonal statements, jackets in modern cuts, statement boots, patterned scarves, bold belts, and on-trend handbags. These pieces keep your look fresh and fashion-forward, while still complementing the minimalist foundation. Fashion trend research, such as that from WGSN (World Global Style Network), shows that integrating just a small percentage of trend-led items into a wardrobe creates visual interest and prevents your style from becoming stagnant. In this book's wardrobe solutions, these trend pieces are where you can apply your seasonal colour palette and experiment with prints and embellishments suited to your body shape.

10% Couture and Formal Attire

Finally, 10% of your wardrobe can be reserved for couture, luxury, or formalwear, investment pieces that you either purchase for specific occasions or gradually collect over time. This may include a tailored evening gown, a bespoke blazer, or heritage-quality footwear. Experts from Parsons School of Design recommend treating these pieces as long-term investments, choosing high-quality materials and craftsmanship that will remain relevant for years. In the styling solutions provided in this book, these pieces often serve as your statement anchors, garments that elevate your look for professional events, special celebrations, or moments when you want to make an unforgettable impression.

How This Works

This 60-30-10 approach ensures that you are never overwhelmed by excess or underprepared for key occasions. The minimalist base supports the daily needs of your lifestyle, the trend-driven elements add vibrancy and keep your look current, and the couture/formal investments provide the polish and drama for special moments. When applied to the body shape dressing principles outlined in each chapter, this philosophy ensures that your wardrobe is not only balanced and stylish but also perfectly tailored to your figure, colouring, and personality, making every outfit feel intentional and empowering.

Essential Pieces for Every Body Shape

While each body type has its styling guidelines, certain essential pieces are versatile enough to work across all shapes and colours. Start with neutral foundation pieces (like black, beige, or navy) that flatter all skin tones. Add splashes of colour using tops, accessories, or outerwear in hues suited to your undertone. For example, a mustard top for warm undertones or a cobalt dress for cool tones can be both flattering and versatile. Here are the must-have basics for a capsule wardrobe that works for everyone, along with tips on choosing the best cuts and styles for your body shape.

1. **Tops**
   - **Fitted Tees and Tanks**: These basics work as layering pieces and are perfect for creating balanced looks. Apple and pear body shapes might go for V-necks to elongate, while hourglass body shapes, athletic body shapes, and strawberry shapes look great in scoop necks.

   - **Blouses with Detail**: Choose blouses with flattering necklines (V-neck, boatneck, or scoop) and subtle details. For pear body shapes, look for blouses with shoulder details; strawberry shapes might prefer more understated tops.

   - **Button-Down Shirts**: A timeless essential that works well tucked into high-waisted jeans or layered under blazers. Go for relaxed fits for athletic body shapes, while hourglass figures might prefer a tailored cut to define the waist.

2. **Bottoms**
   - **High-Waisted Jeans**: Universally flattering and incredibly versatile, high-waisted jeans come in various cuts like straight-leg, flared, and skinny. Each body shape can find a flattering fit. Pear and hourglass shapes benefit from bootcut or straight-leg, while athletic body shapes and apple body shapes might go for a more structured, high-waisted fit.

   - **Tailored Trousers**: Perfect for work or dressier occasions, tailored trousers bring polish to any look. Wide-leg or straight-leg cuts suit most body types, especially when high-waisted to define the waistline.

   - **A-Line Skirts**: This skirt is a capsule wardrobe hero! It flatters every body type by creating balance and adding body shape. Choose knee-length or midi styles in neutral tones or classic prints.

3. **Dresses**
   - **Wrap Dresses**: The ultimate body-type-friendly dress, the wrap dress defines the

waist and flatters every silhouette. Hourglass body shapes, apple body shapes, and pear body shapes look fantastic in wrap styles, while athletic body shapes and strawberry shapes can play with asymmetrical or high-waisted versions.

- o **Shift Dresses**: A versatile, easy-to-style option, shift dresses work well for athletic and apple shapes, as they skim the body without clinging. Adding a belt can create a waistline, making it work for pear and hourglass shapes, too.

- o **A-Line Dresses**: For a feminine, balanced look, A-line dresses are universally flattering and add just the right amount of body shape.

4. **Outerwear**
   - o **Blazers**: Choose blazers that add structure and body shape, such as a single-breasted or slightly tailored blazer. Pear and Strawberry body shapes can benefit from structured shoulders, while hourglass and athletic body shapes might prefer styles that nip in at the waist.

   - o **Trench Coats**: Classic and chic, trench coats add polish to any outfit and work for every body type. Look for ones with a belt to emphasize the waist, and feel free to play with colours and patterns for personality.

   - o **Long Cardigans**: Long cardigans add a soft, relaxed vibe to any outfit and work beautifully for layering. They're especially flattering on athletic and pear body shapes, creating length and soft lines.

5. **Accessories**
   - o **Belts**: A belt is your best friend in a capsule wardrobe, defining the waist and adding interest to any look. Opt for a simple, neutral belt or a statement one for added flair.

   - o **Scarves**: Scarves add warmth, colour, and dimension. Lightweight scarves are great for transitional seasons, while chunky knits are perfect for colder weather.

- Statement Jewellery: A few pieces of statement jewellery, like a bold necklace or oversized earrings, can transform an outfit and add personality to even the simplest basics.

Building Your Capsule Wardrobe by Season

Capsule wardrobes are even more effective when they work year-round. Incorporate scarves, belts, or jewellery to experiment with bold colours if you're hesitant about committing to full garments. Seasonal changes may also influence colour choices like pastels for spring and deeper tones for winter.

This balanced approach to colour ensures your wardrobe highlights your best features, complements your natural beauty, and aligns with your style. Use this as a creative starting point to craft a look that feels and looks great on you.

Here's a breakdown of how to transition your capsule pieces across seasons while dressing for your body type.

1. **Spring & Summer**
   - **Light Layers**: Lightweight jackets, blazers, and cardigans are perfect for spring layering. Choose structured styles if you want to add to your look.

   - **Dresses and Skirts**: Opt for A-line skirts, wrap dresses, and sundresses in breathable fabrics. These pieces are easy to mix and match with tees and blouses, offering endless outfit options for warm weather.

   - **Neutral and Pastel Tones**: The spring and summer months are great for lighter colours. Apple, strawberry and athletic body shapes can go for pastel or patterned skirts to create balance.

1. **Fall & Winter**
   - **Heavy Layers**: In colder months, you'll rely on coats, sweaters, and scarves. Invest in a good trench or wool coat, tailored to flatter your body shape.

- o **Chunky Sweaters**: Choose chunky sweaters in flattering necklines (V-neck, scoop, or turtleneck). Hourglass-shaped bodies look good in belted oversized sweaters, while apple-shaped bodies might prefer loose-fitting sweaters with wider or asymmetrical hems.

- o **Dark and Rich Colours**: Deep colours like burgundy, navy, and forest green add depth and work well with capsule neutrals. Ladies with apple and strawberry-shaped bodies can choose darker colours on top while going for richer and brighter coloured bottoms.

Outfit Formulas for Easy Styling

Once you have your capsule wardrobe, creating outfits becomes a breeze. Here are some go-to outfit formulas that work for each body type:

- **Apple Body Shape Outfit Formula**: V-neck tee + high-waisted jeans + long cardigan + ankle boots.
- **Pear Body Shape Outfit Formula**: Embellished blouse + A-line skirt + statement belt + ballet flats.
- **Hourglass Body Shape Outfit Formula**: Wrap dress + trench coat + pumps + classic jewellery.
- **Athletic Body Shape Outfit Formula**: Fitted top + belted wide-leg pants + blazer + loafers.
- **Strawberry Body Shape Formula**: Scoop-neck top + tiered midi skirt + fitted jacket + sandals.

These combinations take the guesswork out of styling, letting you effortlessly put together polished, body-type-friendly looks.

Curating Quality Over Quantity

The beauty of a capsule wardrobe is that it encourages you to choose quality over quantity. By investing in well-made pieces that suit your body type, you'll find that they last longer, look better, and give you greater satisfaction with every wear. Look for pieces in durable, comfortable fabrics that feel as good as they look. When possible, avoid fast fashion. This will elevate your wardrobe and help you become more sustainable in your fashion and style choices.

Conclusion: Celebrating Your Style Journey

Congratulations on making it to the end of this style journey! If there's one takeaway from this book, let it be this: your style is a celebration of *you*. Every choice you make, whether it's a bold print, a simple silhouette, or a favourite colour, is an expression of who you are and what makes you unique. Embracing your body shape, exploring new looks, and curating a wardrobe that feels authentic to you are all parts of a joyful journey toward self-acceptance and confidence.

Remember, personal style is not about fitting into a mould; it's about finding the pieces that make you feel your best. As you continue to explore your wardrobe and try out new combinations, allow yourself to experiment without pressure. Fashion is meant to be fun, so don't be afraid to play around and discover what resonates most with you.

Celebrate Your Personal Style

This book may be ending, but your journey with style is just beginning! Now that you have the tools to choose fabrics, patterns, colours, and cuts that complement your body shape, you're ready to explore endless outfit possibilities. Don't hesitate to step outside of your comfort zone and try something new, whether it is a new silhouette, a bold colour, or a statement accessory. Each choice is an opportunity to learn more about what makes you feel vibrant and confident.

Celebrate the joy of fashion by expressing your individuality. Let your wardrobe be a place where you find inspiration and creativity every day. Whether you're dressing up for an event, heading to work, or just relaxing at home, each outfit is a chance to embrace your unique style. And always remember, fashion is for *you*. The goal is to feel comfortable and confident in your skin.

As a final thought, consider this: style is not about perfection; it's about presence. So, walk with confidence, wear what makes you happy, and let your wardrobe tell the world your story. Your journey with fashion, self-expression, and self-love is a lifelong adventure. Enjoy every step of the way.

Here's to you and the incredible uniqueness you bring to the world. Keep exploring, keep celebrating, and above all, keep being *you*.

Appendix: Quick Reference Guides

Welcome to the appendix, a handy toolkit you can come back to any time you need a refresher! Here you'll find quick reference guides tailored to each body shape, a glossary of fabrics and patterns, and practical shopping and tailoring tips. Whether you're choosing outfits and fabrics or tackling a shopping trip, these pages are here to make styling easy and fun. Let's dive into the essentials for confident dressing!

Body Shape Tips

Each body shape has its unique style formula. Use these formulas to quickly find outfit ideas and tips tailored to you. These mini guides give you timesaving and essential guidance for choosing looks that celebrate your silhouette and highlight your favourite features. Remember to explore other looks. Nothing is set in stone when building personal style. It is a lifelong, evolving adventure.

1. **Apple Body Shape Style Cheats**
   - **Go-To Outfit Formula**: Dark, fitted V-neck top + bright or patterned A-line skirt or wide-leg pants.

   - **Key Tips**: Keep the upper body sleek with simple lines and add interest with fuller bottoms or bold colours on the lower section of your body.

   - **Essential Fabrics**: Lightweight, flowing fabrics on top, paired with structured bottoms to create balance.

2. **Pear Body Shape Style Cheats**
   - **Go-To Outfit Formula**: Patterned or textured top + high-waisted tailored trousers in dark colours.

   - **Key Tips**: Draw attention upward with interesting tops and keep the lower body streamlined to create balance.

- Essential Fabrics: Structured materials for bottoms and softer, eye-catching fabrics on top.

3. **Hourglass Body Shape Style Cheats**
   - **Go-To Outfit Formula**: Wrap dress or belted blazer + fitted pencil skirt or tailored pants.

   - **Key Tips**: Emphasize the waist and show off balanced curves with fitted pieces that hug the body.

   - **Essential Fabrics**: Stretch fabrics and soft knits that define curves and create smooth lines. For more subtility, use structured fabrics such as cotton and linen.

4. **Athletic Body Shape Style Cheats**
   - **Go-To Outfit Formula**: Layered or textured top + high-waisted, flared jeans or an A-line skirt.

   - **Key Tips**: Add volume and form with textured fabrics, patterns, and layers that bring depth to your look.

   - **Essential Fabrics**: Structured or textured fabrics like linen and tweed to create dimension.

5. **Strawberry Body Shape Style Cheats**
   - **Go-To Outfit Formula**: Dark, tailored top + patterned or ruffled skirt or wide-leg pants.

   - **Key Tips**: Soften the upper body with simple cuts and draw attention to the hips with volume or bold prints on the lower section of your body.

   - **Essential Fabrics**: Loose fabrics on top and structured or textured materials on the lower body.

Fabric and Pattern Glossary

Understanding fabrics and patterns is key to choosing pieces that work with your body shape. This glossary gives you a quick look at different fabrics and patterns, along with suggestions on how to incorporate them into your wardrobe for the best effect.

1. **Fabric Types**
   - **Silk**: Soft and flowy, ideal for creating movement and a touch of luxury. Works well for apple and strawberry body shapes, especially in tops.

   - **Cotton**: Lightweight and breathable, versatile for casual and tailored looks. Suitable for all shapes as a base layer or fitted piece.

   - **Denim**: Durable and structured, great for adding form and structure. Perfect for athletic and hourglass body shape bottoms.

   - **Linen**: Light and textured, giving an effortless vibe with added dimension. Wonderful for athletic body shapes to add form without clinging.

   - **Jersey**: Soft and stretchy, ideal for fitted looks that hug the body. Perfect for hourglass body shapes in dresses and fitted tops.

2. **Pattern Types**
   - **Stripes**

   Vertical stripes are excellent for elongating the figure and creating a streamlined silhouette, making them ideal for wide-leg pants or longline blouses—especially flattering for athletic and apple body shapes. Horizontal stripes add visual width and volume and can be used strategically to balance proportions—particularly on pear body shapes, where a striped top can draw attention upward. For subtle sophistication, consider pinstripes, chalk stripes, or broken stripes on tailored pieces for a touch of modern refinement.

- **Floral Prints**

  Floral patterns can soften angular features and add a feminine or romantic touch to any ensemble. Small florals work beautifully on hourglass and athletic shapes when printed on refined fabrics like silk crepe or cotton sateen. Larger floral prints create volume and are especially flattering for apple and pear body shapes, particularly when placed on skirts or dresses. For elegance, choose monochromatic, watercolour, or photographic florals on luxurious bases like chiffon, silk, or velvet. Jewel-toned or muted palettes elevate florals from casual to couture.

- **Polka Dots**

  Classic and playful, polka dots can enhance curves and create visual energy. Medium- to large-scale dots on skirts or dresses are flattering for strawberry and athletic shapes, while micro polka dots in soft colours can add whimsy without overwhelming petite frames. For a timeless, elegant touch, choose dots on structured silk or matte cotton blends in navy, ivory, or black.

- **Plaids and Checks**

  Structured and bold, plaid and check patterns add dimension and can sharpen or ground a look. They are ideal for athletic body shapes and apple body shapes, especially when worn on tailored jackets or trousers. Opt for plaid, windowpane, or houndstooth checks in neutral or tonal colorways for an elevated, heritage-inspired effect. Lightweight wools, tweeds, or brushed cottons lend sophistication to these classic motifs.

- **Animal Prints**

  Eye-catching and dynamic, animal prints are ideal for making a statement and showcasing confidence. They work particularly well for hourglass and pear shapes when used on tops, skirts, or statement outerwear.

To keep the look luxurious, select tone-on-tone leopard, python embossing, or faux croc patterns in rich fabrics like silk, jacquard, or velvet. Use sparingly or balance with neutrals for a polished finish.

Bonus Pattern Types to Explore:

- **Damask Patterns**: Inspired by traditional woven motifs, damask adds historical richness and grandeur. Best used in formalwear or statement pieces, especially for evening looks. Try it on silk, satin, or jacquard to enhance elegance.

- **Subtle Geometrics**: Minimalist yet refined, these include latticework, micro-diamonds, and tonal tessellations. Excellent for workwear and modern separates. Pair with clean silhouettes on fine cotton, crepe, or wool-blend garments.

- **Delicate Embroidery & Lace Overlays**: Use embroidered tulle, Chantilly lace, or tonal thread work to add romantic elegance. These elements work beautifully on structured garments or layered dresses and flatter every shape when thoughtfully placed.

Fabric Patterns Gallery: Creative Inspiration & Resources

Images of different fabric types and patterns are available for purchase through my website in case you are a clever, creative.

STRIPES

SANCTUARY
A soft ivory base anchored by calm black & taupe vertical stripes.

SEABOUND
A timeless navy & white horizontal stripe with bold contrast.

SLATE
Modern minimalism & precision. Fine vertical stripes in grey and white.

NIGHTFALL
A luxe midnight navy softened by whisper-thin pinstripes.

FLORALS

CELESTIALS
A dreamy blend of muted gold and silvery blue florals.

MORNING DEW
Soft blush & lavender blossoms bloom across a delicate lilac base.

GOLDEN BLOOM
Luminous golden lilies bloom over a rich charcoal canvas.

CELESTIAL SENTINEL
Tall luminous lillies stand poised like guardians on a chocolate base.

POLKA DOTS

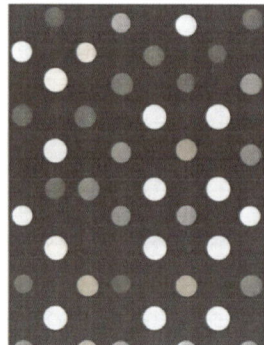

CLASSIC POP
Bold, high-contrast black dots on crisp white. A punchy statement with vintage charm.

ROSE DOTS
Soft & romantic. Pale blush backdrop sprinkled with delicate white dots.

MODERN BALANCE
A medley of white, beige, & grey dots rests on a charcoal base.

GILDED RHYTHM
Shimmering gold & silver polka dots on deep black linen texture.

PLAIDS & CHECKS

THE ALISON
Soft lilac, dusty grey, & shimmering gold plaid. Demur.

MINT HERITAGE
A refreshing mix of mint & rose pink woven with gold threads.

HARVEST GOLD
Earthy brown tones meets gold in a plaid re-imagined with rustic charm.

CLASSIC REVIVAL
A bold contrast of black & white softened by gold pinstripes.

DAMASK

COVENANT
Radiating symmetry in gold & pewter hues, evoking unity, & divine design.

BAROQUE GRACE
A regal damask pattern in antique gold & silver across a charcoal backdrop.

KINGDOM BLOOM
Ornate golden damask pattern over deep sapphire blue.

DIVINE HEIRLOOM
Celestial feather-like damask motifs in luminous lavender & gold.

EMBROIDERY

GOLDEN GRACE
Delicate gold floral embroidery climbs across a luminescent base.

GOLDEN TAPESTRY
Rich golden leaves and blossoms etched into blush-toned tulle.

WHISPER
Ivory & black embroidery trace an organic vine on pearl-toned satin.

NIGHT BLOOM
Crisp silver floral embroidery blooms against deep black fabric.

Shopping and Tailoring Tips

1. **Shopping Strategies**
   - **Know Your Must-Have Fits**: Having a go-to list of fits (like A-line skirts for Pear body shapes or wrap tops for hourglass body shapes) helps streamline your shopping and avoids unnecessary purchases.

   - **Choose Versatile Pieces**: Look for items that can be dressed up or down, layered, and easily mixed. This will make your wardrobe adaptable and simplify outfit creation.

   - **Quality Over Quantity**: Investing in well-made essentials will serve you better in the long run. Choose high-quality basics that fit well and feel good on your skin.

2. **Tailoring Tips for the Perfect Fit**
   - **Hem Adjustments**: The right hem length can completely change how a piece looks on your body. Shorten skirts or dresses to a length that complements your body shape, and ensure pants fit at the most flattering point for your body shape.

   - **Waist Cinching**: A simple waist adjustment can enhance your form by creating a more defined silhouette. This is especially effective for hourglass and Athletic body shapes.

   - **Shoulder Adjustments**: If shoulders are too wide, it can throw off the balance of the entire outfit. Adjusting the shoulders can make tops fit better for strawberry and apple body shapes. Neatly rolling up your sleeves to a ¾ length can enhance your top's balance.

   - **Darts and Seams**: Adding darts or seams can contour a garment to your body, making it more flattering. Great for blazers, dresses, and button-down shirts for all shapes.

3. **Practical Tips for Online Shopping**
   o **Check Measurements Carefully**: Different brands have different sizing, so always check the brand's specific measurements. This is especially helpful for finding the right fit for your body shape.

   o **Read Reviews**: Many reviewers will comment on fit and fabric. Look for feedback that has similar themes to get a realistic idea of how the piece might look on you.

   o **Know What to Look For**: If you're trying to enhance certain features, prioritize cuts, colours, and fabrics that work for your body shape. Have a checklist of your "body shape-friendly" pieces for reference.

This quick-reference guide is designed to be a resource that you can come back to when needed. Whether you're heading to the store, choosing new outfits, or updating your wardrobe staples, these tips will keep you feeling confident, empowered, and stylish.

With these tools at your fingertips, you're ready to take on any styling challenge and make every look uniquely yours. Embrace the journey, enjoy each discovery, and remember, your style is a celebration of *you*. Also, check out our mini-guides and shopping guide for each body shape on our website.

Final Thoughts

Personal style is an ever-evolving reflection of our preferences and perceptions. Your preferences and perceptions may change over time, and that's part of the beauty of this journey. What you loved wearing last year might look different today, and tomorrow's style might surprise you! Embrace these changes with an open heart. Style is fluid, and as you grow, your wardrobe grows with you.

Self-acceptance is the foundation of great style. When you love and accept yourself, it radiates through every outfit you put on. Remember that every body shape is beautiful and deserves to be celebrated. Your body shape is not something to "fix" or "hide"; it's something to enhance and embrace because it's uniquely yours. With each piece you add to your wardrobe, let it remind you of your worth, beauty, and individuality.

About the Author

Audra is a stylist, retired model, author, and founder of Style By Audra. With a background in modelling, personal styling, and social work, she empowers women to dress with purpose, confidence, and authenticity. Her fashion philosophy blends minimalist structure with expressive detail, offering timeless guidance for real bodies and everyday life.

Through her books, blog, and social media channels, Audra helps readers discover their unique shape, organise their wardrobe, and elevate their brand, nurturing and empowering them from the inside out. When she's not writing, styling, or creating content, you'll find her immersed in nature, exploring holistic wellness.

To collaborate with Audra or to find more guides on fashion and style, visit stylebyaudra.com

"BEYOND THE ART, MY FAITH INSPIRES EVERYTHING I DO. IT FUELS MY DESIRE TO CREATE WORKS THAT RESONATE WITH OTHERS, WHETHER THROUGH A POWERFUL IMAGE, A MEANINGFUL LYRIC, OR A TRANSFORMATIVE STORY. I BELIEVE ART HAS THE ABILITY TO BRING BEAUTY AND HOPE INTO THE WORLD."

AUDRA OAKES

FASHION
REIMAGINED

A Gallery of Realistic AI Generated Models & Prompts

AUDRA OAKES

FASHION
REIMAGINED

A Gallery of Realistic AI Generated Models & Prompts

ISBN: 978-1-7640606-2-2
First Edition
Printed in Australia

Table of Contents

Dedication

To my mother,
When I did not know what clothes were, you bought
me my first matching sets. You instilled in me a
love for creativity, beauty, and elegance that
has shaped my journey in life and in fashion. I
Love You.

This book is also dedicated to every creative
soul who dares to re-imagine the world. May you
find inspiration, courage, and joy in crafting
something new and meaningful.

May your dreams be woven into reality, one
stitch, one sketch, and one word at a time.

Introduction

Welcome to the world of Fashion Reimagined, where creativity meets cutting-edge technology. This book is your guide to incorporating Artificial Intelligence into your fashion and design workflow, offering innovative ways to reduce costs, minimize waste, and enhance efficiency. Whether you're a creative professional, freelancer, or sole proprietor, this journey will help you transform your ideas into tangible, breathtaking designs.

Why Reimagine Fashion?

Fashion is more than clothing; it's a statement, a story, and an art form. With the rise of AI, we now have tools to take our creative visions to new heights. By using AI effectively, you can:

- Streamline your workflow by visualizing finished products before investing in production.
- Reduce costs through smarter planning and resource allocation.
- Enhance sustainability by minimizing waste and embracing innovation.

What to Expect

This book is not about replacing human creativity but enhancing it. Each chapter introduces a design concept, accompanied by the tools and AI-generated visuals that bring it to life. You'll learn:

- How to integrate AI tools like ChatGPT and MidJourney into your workflow.
- Practical prompts and tips to achieve stunning results.
- Strategies for balancing human input with AI efficiency.

A Personal Touch

The designs in this book are deeply personal, many inspired by my experiences growing up in Liberia, Ghana, and Italy. Through AI, I've been able to revive and reimagine sketches from decades ago, giving them new life and purpose. This book is as much about my journey as it is about yours—a shared exploration of creativity and possibility.

A Note on AI

There's no reason to fear AI when you understand its potential. Like any tool, its value lies in how we use it. AI can free up time for what matters most—spending time with loved ones, pursuing passions, and creating a better future. However, like any invention, it can be misused. Let's choose to wield this powerful tool responsibly, with creativity, purpose, and integrity.

An Invitation to Create

Fashion Reimagined is an interactive experience. The prompts and strategies shared here are adaptable—change them, refine them, and make them your own. Think of this book as a starting point, a conversation about how we can use technology to build a more creative and sustainable world.

With that, let's dive into the fun, exciting, and sometimes surprising world of AI-powered design. Together, let's reimagine what's possible.

CHAPTER ONE

Process Overview

Unlocking Creativity with AI Tools

In the world of Fashion Reimagined, every design begins with a spark of inspiration and evolves into a polished masterpiece through a blend of traditional artistry and cutting-edge technology. This chapter provides a universal overview of the methods and tools used in the book, offering a practical guide to replicating these processes for your own creative projects. Whether you're starting with a sketch, a concept, or pure imagination, this process will show you how to harness AI to bring your designs to life.

1. Starting Point: Sketch, Vision, or Idea

Every creation begins differently. Here are the three main starting points I've used:

- Sketch-Based Designs: Hand-drawn sketches served as the foundation for many designs in this book, each infused with personal history and creative passion.
- Direct AI-Driven Concepts: Some designs were brought to life solely through imaginative prompting, leveraging AI to visualize ideas that existed only in my mind.
- Hybrid Workflow: A combination of hand-drawn sketches and iterative AI enhancements was used to refine complex ideas into polished designs.

2. Tools of the Trade

The two primary AI tools that made this journey possible are:

- MidJourney: A versatile tool for generating high-quality, photorealistic visuals. It excels at translating detailed prompts into stunning designs.
- NewArc AI: Used as an intermediate step for some sketches, this tool enhances basic drawings, setting the stage for further refinement in MidJourney.

Additional tools like Canva and photo editing software were used to fine-tune the final outputs, ensuring every image met professional standards.

3. The Creative Workflow

Regardless of the starting point, the process generally follows these steps:

Step 1: Preparing the Input

- **For Sketch-Based Designs:**
  - Photograph or scan your hand-drawn sketch.
  - Upload the sketch to NewArc AI for initial enhancement and transformation into a digital render.
  - Export the enhanced image to refine further in MidJourney.
- **For AI-Driven Concepts:**
  - Start with a clear mental image of your design. Write down descriptive details, including style, texture, color palette, and mood.
  - Develop a prompt that captures your vision as precisely as possible.
  - Use MidJourney to bring your idea to life directly from the prompt.

Step 2: Writing Effective Prompts

Prompts are the heart of AI-generated designs. Here's how to craft them effectively:

- Be Specific: Include details about the design elements, such as fabric type, colors, patterns, and style (e.g., "sleek black bob hairstyle, diamond-patterned sheer gown, high collar neckline, form-fitting silhouette, side slit").
- Define the Mood and Context: Specify whether the design is for a fashion editorial, runway, or casual wear.
- Experiment with Parameters: Use MidJourney parameters like --ar (aspect ratio) and --v (version) to refine the output.

Step 3: Iterative Refinement

- Review the AI-generated image and identify areas for improvement (e.g., lighting, contrast, or design details).
- Use updated prompts or manual adjustments to fine-tune the result until it matches your vision.

Step 4: Post-Production

- Download the final AI-generated image.
- Enhance the image using tools like Canva for adjustments to lighting, contrast, brightness, or resolution.
- If creating a portfolio or book, ensure consistent formatting and professional presentation.

4. Adapting the Process

Creativity is not one-size-fits-all. While this process worked for my designs, it can be tailored to suit your workflow. For instance:

- Skip the sketching phase and start directly with prompts if you're more comfortable with digital tools.
- Use other AI platforms to explore features not available in MidJourney or NewArc AI.

5. Tips for Success

- **Test and Iterate:** Don't expect perfection on the first try. Experiment with different prompts and settings.
- **Embrace Collaboration:** Share your designs with peers or mentors for feedback and suggestions.
- **Document Your Journey**: Keep a record of prompts, tools, and iterations for reference and learning.

This universal process is designed to inspire and guide your own creative journey. Whether you're working with cherished sketches from the past or dreaming up new ideas, AI tools can help you bring your vision to life with precision, creativity, and efficiency. The key is to stay curious, adaptable, and bold in your exploration of what's possible. Now, let's move forward and dive deeper into how each design in this book came to life.

CHAPTER TWO

Obsidian Elegance

Obsidian Elegance – From Sketch to AI Realization

Every design has a story, and for me, "Obsidian Elegance" represents the beginning of my journey in fashion. Inspired by my time in Ghana and Rome, this chapter explores how a pencil sketch from 1997 was transformed into a stunning, AI-rendered design.

You'll learn about the tools, prompts, and process that brought this vision to life. This chapter highlights how AI can resurrect creative ideas from the past and refine them for the future.

Obsidian Elegance was sketched in 1998. This elegant design was refined with Midjourney in 2024.

Figure 1: Obsidian Elegance

CHAPTER THREE

Dark Royal

Dark Royal – The Drama of Style

Fashion is a form of storytelling, and "Dark Royal" tells a tale of bold elegance and theatrical flair. Inspired by the grandeur of tango dancers, this chapter delves into how AI can enhance dramatic designs while maintaining their classic charm. Through step-by-step insights, you'll discover how to use AI tools to add depth, realism, and personality to your creations.

Dark Royal was sketched in 1998 and brought to life using NewArc. I fine tuned the using Midjourney in 2024.

Figure 3: Dark Royal

CHAPTER FOUR

Lady in Grey

Lady in Grey – Merging Vision with Practicality

In "Lady in Grey," we explore the intersection of imagination and execution. This design reflects my journey as a writer and thinker who visualizes in images but communicates through words. In this chapter, I'll show how AI can bridge the gap between raw sketches and fully realized concepts, offering a practical framework for turning visions into reality.

Figure 5: Lady In Grey

CHAPTER FIVE

Vivid Vogue

Vivid Vogue – Celebrating Color and Youth

"Vivid Vogue" is a celebration of energy, vibrancy, and youthful creativity. While I personally lean towards muted tones, this design pays homage to the bold colors and daring ideas of my younger self. This chapter demonstrates how AI can bring playful, vibrant designs to life, encouraging you to step out of your comfort zone and embrace experimentation.

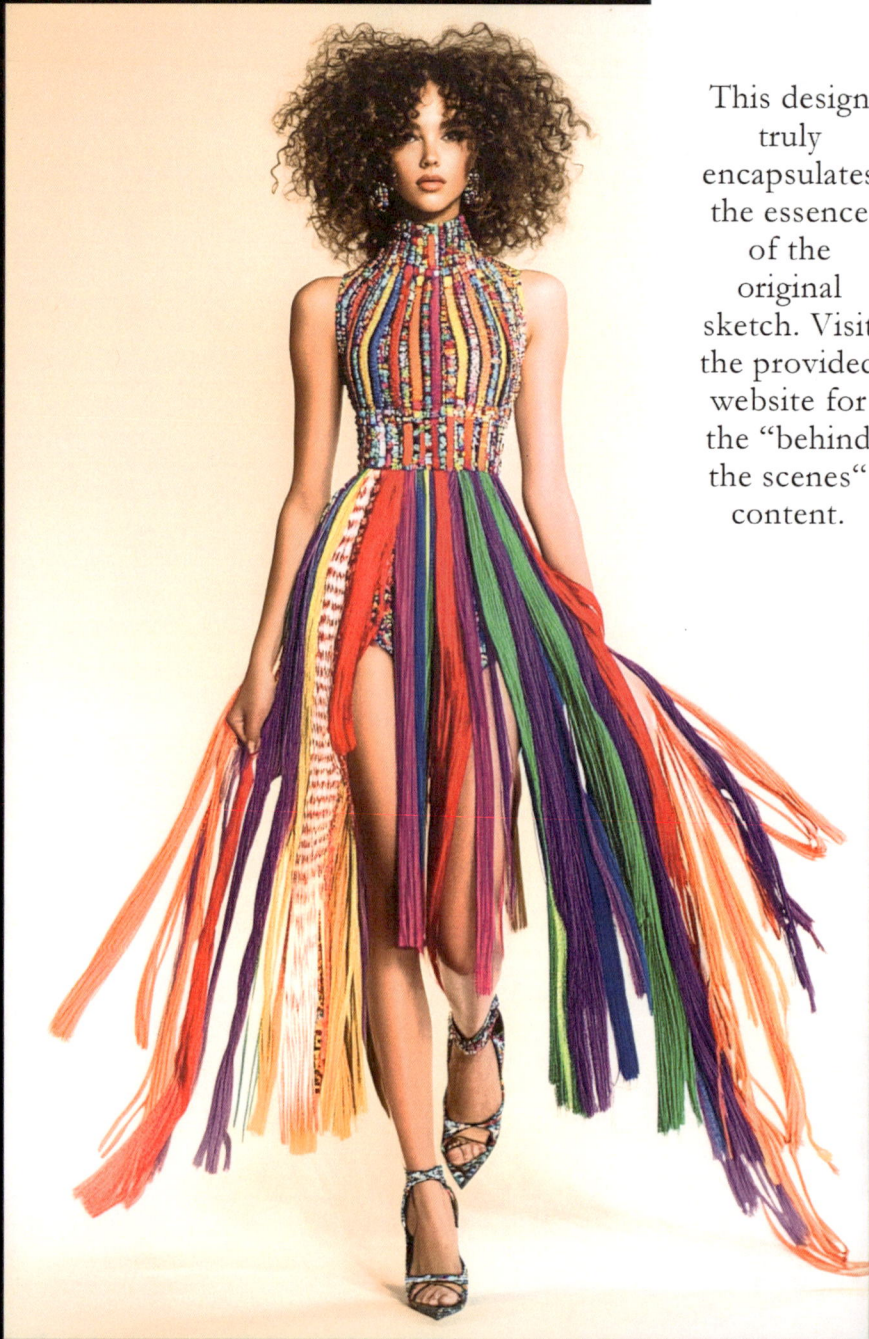

This design truly encapsulates the essence of the original sketch. Visit the provided website for the "behind the scenes" content.

Figure 6: Vivid Vogue

CHAPTER SIX

Sahara Silhouette

Sahara Silhouette – A Tribute to Timeless Elegance

In the heart of fashion lies the ability to evoke emotions, tell stories, and connect deeply with cultural and natural inspirations. "Sahara Silhouette" is a celebration of elegance shaped by the warm tones and endless horizons of the desert. This design combines flowing lines and earthy hues, drawing inspiration from the shifting sands and radiant sunsets of the Sahara.

This design highlights the power of simplicity and precision in design. From the initial concept to its breathtaking final form, Sahara Silhouette exemplifies how AI tools can transform a vision into a masterpiece. The seamless interplay of stripes and earthy colors reflects a balance between boldness and grace, reminding us that the beauty of nature can inspire innovation in unexpected ways.

Sahara
Silhouette
was sketched
in 1998
originally.
Visit the
provided
website for
the "behind
the scenes"
content.

Figure 8: Sahara Silhouettee

Christmas Style Inspiration

Step into the festive season with elegance and creativity! The Christmas Style Inspiration gallery showcases AI-generated designs that blend the warmth of holiday traditions with modern sophistication. From shimmering evening gowns to cozy yet chic ensembles, these designs are perfect for celebrating in style. Let the vibrant colors, intricate details, and festive themes spark your imagination and help you reimagine your holiday wardrobe.

African Style
INSPIRATION

African Style Inspiration

Drawing from my West African
heritage, the African Style Inspiration
gallery celebrates the vibrant artistry
and cultural pride of African-inspired
fashion. These designs honor
traditional patterns, bold colors, and
timeless silhouettes, reimagined
through the lens of AI creativity. Each
piece reflects the beauty and richness
of African traditions blended with
modern elegance. Let these creations
inspire your journey into fashion that is
both deeply personal and
breathtakingly innovative.

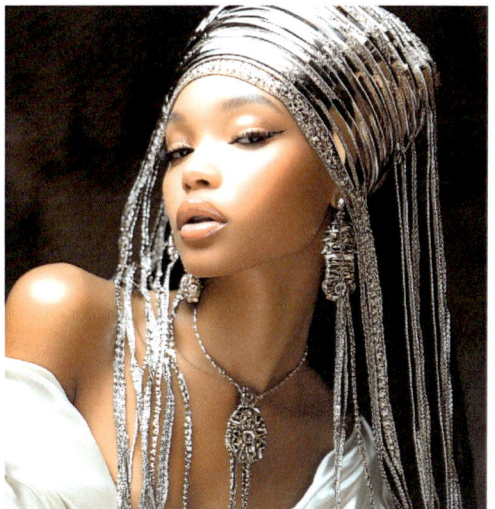

Concept Fashion
INSPIRATION

Concept Fashion Inspiration

Dive into the future of fashion with the Concept Fashion Inspiration gallery, where imagination meets innovation. This collection showcases bold, avant-garde designs that push the boundaries of creativity, blending artistic expression with AI-driven precision. These pieces are not just fashion—they're statements of vision and possibility. Explore the unexpected and be inspired to dream beyond the conventional.

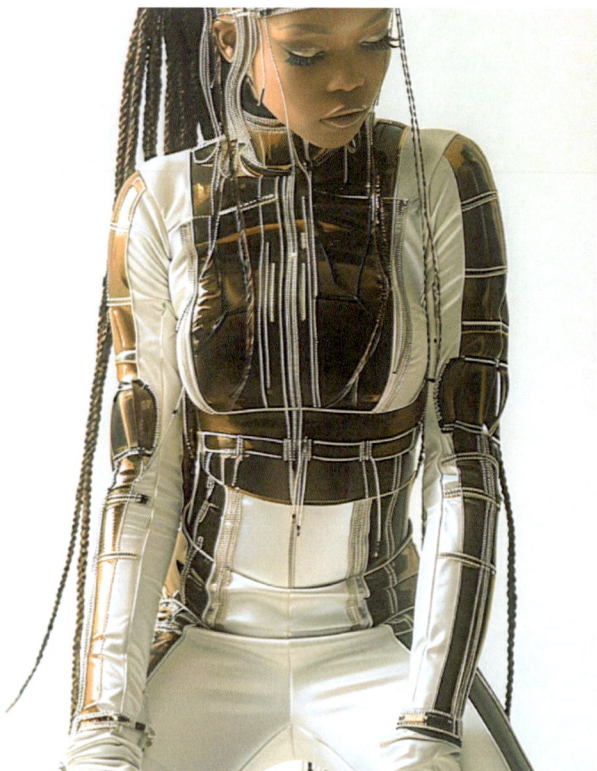

ABOUT

AUDRA

Audra Oakes is an accomplished author, retired model, and creative visionary with a deep passion for fashion and innovation. With years of experience in styling and running an online clothing brand, Audra combines her expertise in design with cutting-edge technology to inspire others.

Her journey in fashion began as a model and stylist, where she cultivated an eye for elegance, form, and sustainability. Today, she leverages Artificial Intelligence to reimagine traditional workflows, making fashion design more accessible, efficient, and environmentally friendly.

Audra's work reflects her commitment to empowering creatives and entrepreneurs to embrace technology while staying true to their artistic roots. Through her books and designs, she invites readers to explore the possibilities of merging human creativity with AI, building a future where innovation meets artistry.

Discover more about Audra's journey and creations in Fashion Reimagined: A Gallery of Realistic AI Generated Models & Prompts, a testament to her dedication to transforming ideas into breathtaking realities.

www.ingramcontent.com/pod-product-compliance
Lightning Source LLC
Chambersburg PA
CBRC101139030426
42338CB00021B/1645